Real Estate Investing in
New York City

Real Estate Investing in New York City

A Handbook for the Small Investor

Robert L. Lewis

iUniverse, Inc.
New York Lincoln Shanghai

Real Estate Investing in New York City
A Handbook for the Small Investor

iUniverse, Inc.

For information address:
iUniverse, Inc.
2021 Pine Lake Road, Suite 100
Lincoln, NE 68512
www.iuniverse.com

ISBN: 0-595-27742-X

Contents

INTRODUCTION

This book is intended for the individual living within or near New York City (or for that matter any urban area) who is seeking to get his or feet wet in real estate. It is not intended for those individuals who are looking to real estate for a new career or who are seeking to make a million dollars there. It is intended for the small businessman or employee who has extra funds to invest and prefers to put them in real estate than in a bank account or in the stock market.

Investing in real estate offers many avenues of approach to the investor. Alternatives are available which require active participation while other approaches require no participation whatsoever. He can seek out extremely safe investments or he can choose those carrying the most risk. As with any investment, the choice is that of the investor. Real estate offers several advantages, which are only available in a few other forms of investment. Real estate can offer a hedge against inflation, tax benefits and leverage. Real estate by its very nature deals with physical assets as opposed to paper assets. Generally speaking, a real estate investment consists of an investment in land and buildings. After you have made your purchase of physical assets, any decrease in the purchasing power of the dollar will only help to increase the worth of your investment. If you are receiving rent from your property, and it is not subject to a long-term lease, you will be free to raise the rent to compensate for any decrease in the purchasing power of the dollar.

Lately, there has been a rush to invest in the so-called "Tangibles," Rather than keep their wealth in paper; people are purchasing real goods such as gold coins, colonial paintings, and antique firearms. These investments do not produce any income and cost money to maintain. Real estate, however, can produce an income while you still own the physical asset. Real estate has traditionally been a source of tax benefits to investors. Other than land, you are entitled to depreciate the value of your investment over the useful economic life of the property. At one time it was assumed that as the property got older it became worth less and less. Today, because of increasing inflation, property has tended to increase rather than decrease in value. For example, older brownstones on the West Side of Manhattan have shown a remarkable increase in value over the part few years rather than declining in value because of their age. Even though real estate may increase in value, the investor is allowed to reduce his ordinary income each year, by an amount, which represents a reasonable estimate of the deterioration of the property. Many investors have depreciated property so that on a tax basis, their investment in the property is now recorded at zero, even though the property is worth substantially more than what they paid for it.

Lastly, real estate offers the opportunity for the investor to borrow money to help finance his purchase price. Rather than having to come up with the whole purchase price himself, he can seek financing for the bulk of the purchase. With the use of financing, the investor can control more assets that he would normally have been able to purchase with only his own money. This is called leverage.

INTRODUCTION

This book developed through the course that I taught at the Baruch School of Business of the City University of the City of New York. The course is entitled "Investing in Real Estate." Some of my students are elderly individuals who are first turning to real estate while others are young men who have barely graduated from high school. Some of the people enrolled in the course are wealthy while others are poor. Some have a substantial income while others are barely able to support themselves. I have had students with M.B.A.s from Harvard while others in my class have only a High School Equivalency Diploma. My student body can be broken down into various categories.

THE SUBSTANTIAL INVESTOR

Some of the people taking my course have made a lot of money through their businesses and professions. They are now preparing to retire or ease off. They look to real estate as an alternate form of investing in conjunction with other investments in bonds and stocks. These investors are not looking to make a killing, but rather to conserve whatever money have previously earned. They tend to very conservative in their outlook and are not seeking to be actively involved in management. In speaking to them, many regard their Florida Condominiums, which they use during their winter vacations, as a form of investment.

THE SUBSTANTIAL EARNER

Another portion of my student body consists of businessmen and professionals who are earning substantial sums of money and are seeking to make tax advantaged investments so that the government will take less of a bite from their incomes. These individuals are primarily middle aged and have experienced some degree of success in their occupations. I have had dentists, advertising executives, attorneys, sweat shirt manufacturers, retail storeowners and stockbrokers. These individuals are seeking to make investments which will grow as time passes. They are presently not looking for current income from their investments but rather a means of accumulating money over the intermediate future. They are interested in real estate as it offers them some tax shelter. They are heavily taxed on their present earnings and any ordinary investments they make will only add to their tax burden. Investing in real estate gives them the opportunity of sheltering the income to be received from their new investment and even, sometimes, sheltering part of their earned incomes. Although some of them have a substantial income from their business or profession, most do not have any substantial ready cash available for investment. It seems that their standard of living and the government take all their excess money from them. These individuals are seeking to accumulate a small amount of money so that they may use it in making investments. The money so generated will in turn be further invested.

THE "BREAKOUT" INVESTOR

Others in my course neither earned substantial sums from their business or profession nor had they accumulated any great sums of money. These are individuals who have average or even below average jobs and have little expectation for improving their positions in life through their jobs or existing businesses. They look upon investing in real estate as a way of enhancing their future and improving their lives. Many of these individuals are clerks with the City, schoolteachers, secretaries and factory employees. They do not have the necessary skills with which to improve their position in the job market. They do not have a lot of money to buy bonds or stocks and obtain substantial additional income. All they have in common is the willingness to work hard and to try and build a dream. They look on real estate as a means of achieving this goal. With the leverage offered by real estate, they have the possibility with a small investment and hard labor, of making their investment grow and prosper. These individuals are not seeking the easy way out, but rather they are looking for the means of developing themselves and achieving something in their lives. They look upon real estate as a means of overcoming the mediocrity which has overtaken their lives.

Throughout the sessions in the course I teach, I am besieged with questions after the lecturing is completed. Many of my students stay as much as an hour after the course, to discuss their goals and problems with me. Some of them are merely seeking answers to specific problems while others are seeking assurances that they will not fail in their proposed new ventures. I try to give the best and most honest advice I can. No one can foresee the future and all investments imply some degree of risk. There is one question common to each class. Throughout the course I am continually asked to recommend some basic book to which they can refer in determining how to get started in real estate. They all want a simple short book, which will clearly spell out the problems, which they may face and which offers basis simple solutions. At first, I tried to find them such a book. Many of the texts I found were far too complicated and too involved. The texts were extremely informative and excellently written, but did not serve their basic needs. These texts were suitable for later use, after the student had begun to get more involved in real estate. They were not suitable as basic texts.

Other books had nice snappy titles and told the reader how to make a million dollar in real estate within one year or how to retire on your real estate investments in six month. These books were written for gullible people seeking get rich schemes and were not suitable for the serious investor starting out in real estate. Many of the comments contained in these books were misleading or completely incorrect.

My students were not concerned with making a million dollars in one year; they were concerned about getting started on a serious enterprise, which would continue for many years. It is out of my student's need for a basic book, that I have written this text. The text itself, is based primarily upon my class lecture, and if it rambles it is because I also ramble as a teacher. The book is not meant to answer every question concerning real estate, but it is intended to provide basic guidelines for the decisions faced by the initial investor rather than offering simple solutions. Once the beginner is aware of the problem or decision, he or she must then proceed to find his or her own solution. This book does not replace the need for outside advice for the beginning investor. One should always consult with real estate brokers, lawyers and accountants before beginning such a venture. The book is designed to bring to the attention of the novice the sorts of problems he should be discussing with experts.

It is my firmest hope that this book will provide impetus and encouragement to the beginner in making his first real estate investment.

COMMON MISCONCEPTIONS

There are four basic misconceptions, which most people have in contemplating a real estate investment. It is these misconceptions which have held back the great majority of people from making investments in real estate. These misconceptions are so ingrained that they are almost taken for granted. It is necessary for the novice investor in real estate not only to overcome these misconceptions, but also to understand completely why they are incorrect. Once this burden is removed from his thinking, the beginner should be able to proceed and make his initial investment in real estate.

YOU HAVE TO BE RICH TO OWN REAL ESTATE

Many people are under the impression that real estate investing is only for the rich. They read in the newspapers about the sale of office buildings or shopping centers for substantial sums of money and believe that these are totally beyond their reach. There is no question that a $100,000,000 office building is beyond the reach of the beginning investor, however, there are many other suitable investments.

Contrary to popular opinion, the purchase of most real estate does not require a substantial outlay of funds. Although you may not be able to buy a prime high-rise apartment in a top neighborhood in the City, it is very possible to purchase a small walk-up (building without elevator) or a pre-war (constructed prior to World War II) apartment house in a marginal area of the City. Many of these apartment houses are sold for low cash with the purchaser taking back a mortgage. These buildings may be in decent shape with a solid tenancy. They do not offer the glamour of a Park Avenue or Sutton Place, but dollar for dollar many of them are equally productive financially. You may not be able to purchase a large enclosed regional shopping center, but you can purchase a small building having one or two stores with two or three apartments above the stores. The tenants occupying the stores may not have the national reputation of a Home Depot or Wal-Mart but they too, can be solid and successful. It should be noted that several years ago W.T. Grant, a leading department store chain, with hundreds of stores throughout the country went into bankruptcy and eventually was completely liquidated. A local neighborhood store, which has been in business in the same neighborhood for many years, on the other hand, can represent a substantial and solid tenancy. The percentage dollar return from a small investment in a neighborhood store with apartments above can be equal to the return of the owner of a large shopping center.

IT TAKES A LONG TIME BEFORE YOU REALIZE A RETURN ON YOUR INVESTMENT

Many people believe that real estate can only be a long-term investment. If you buy a piece of property, you must wait years and years before you begin showing a decent return on your money or before the property substantially appreciates. This is not so. Many people are able to purchase property which will immediately show a substantially return on their investment. It is possible to purchase property where leases are expiring shortly and to obtain substantially increased rentals on the new leases. In addition, many areas of the City are going through rapid change and there is a strong chance for immediate appreciation in your investment.

Even more common than the above, is the fact that many people are able to but property which will show them a 10, 15 or even 20% immediate return on their investment. With the tax benefits in slow appreciation, this can work out to a 25 to 30% annual return on investment. Purchasing real estate is different from purchasing a bond. It is possible for your income to grow larger each year, earning an immediate 10 % return on your investment which can increase to 25 or 50%. In addition, the return will not be totally taxed by the government as you are entitled to take depreciation.

In general, the price of new construction has been increasing dramatically each year. As time passes, it costs more and more to build new buildings. The fact that the building you purchase is already in existence makes its replacement each year become more and more expensive. Even if the area in which you have purchased does not materially improve, the continually increasing cost of construction may add value to your building each and every year.

ONLY THE RICH CAN BORROW MONEY

I have to agree that only someone who has a lot of money can borrow substantial sums. Still, almost anyone can borrow some money. In financing a real estate investment, banks will lend a certain amount of money on almost any property. Depending upon the property and on the purchaser, the banks will either lend a lot or a little money. You cannot expect, immediately, to be able to borrow a million dollars from a bank. But borrowing money from banks is not at all difficult.

Almost everyone has borrowed money from a bank in the form of a credit card or overdrawing on your checking account balance. Banks do not question where that money is going. By using even these two sources of credit from one or several banks, it can be possible to borrow a sufficient sum of money to make your initial purchase in real estate. Many banks will allow you to overdraw your checking account up to the sum of $25,000. In addition, banks are making installment loans of up to $75,000 available to individuals. You may not need the credit qualifications to be able to borrow $5,000, or $15,000 without a problem. This sum plus other money you may be able to borrow from friends or relatives, or from savings, could be sufficient for your real estate investment. Many initial investments have come from furniture loans, home improvement loans, or vacation loans from banks, which funds have been used for making the down payment.

If you are comtemplating buying a one, two or three family house as your initial investment, many banks will give great consideration to giving you a mortgage to make the purchase. The amount of the mortgage may equal to 60%, or even as high as 90%, of the total purchase price. These mortgages are for long periods of time and you will be required to make monthly payments. However, banks are in general, extremely hesitant in granting mortgages on small commercial buildings and apartment houses. They prefer to give mortgages on large commercial or residential buildings or on one, two or three family homes which will be owner occupied.

Another source of borrowing, normally readily available, is from the seller of the property itself. It is very common for the seller to grant the purchaser, a "purchase money mortgage" for the purpose of inducing him to make the purchase. A seller may be asking $200,000 for a building. However, he may be prepared to take back a $150,000 ten-year mortgage. By "taking back" a $150,000 mortgage, the purchaser will only need to come up with $50,000 to make the purchase. This type of financing is also found in the sale of a business where the seller takes back notes secured by the assets of the business.

ONLY PRIME PROPERTIES INCREASE IN VALUE

Many people believe that you have to buy only prime properties if you are going to make a lot of money on your investment. If the property is not located in a prime section of town then it will not appreciate in value.

This is not true. Many people have made fortunes by buying marginal properties, which have become substantial generators of cash flow. Not only can you purchase properties in marginal areas for more reasonable prices but, in general, there is less competition for these types of properties. Everyone wants to buy an apartment house on the Upper East Side of Manhattan but few people are willing to venture into outlying areas of the City. There is no question that buying properties in a marginal area involves more work and aggravation than buying a prime piece of property, but then a greater return may also be available. The purchase of a small commercial building "with" or "occupied by" non-rated (someone without a credit history) tenants may in fact, be more stable and profitable than buying a building containing highly rated tenants who are more demanding about service and who may be also subject to financial reversals. A prosperous merchant on a business street in an outlying area may be as stable as a highly rated corporate client. Everyone wants to own a large office building in the center of the City or a shopping center, which serves the entire region and has stores like Saks Fifth Avenue and Bloomingdale's. Fewer people are willing to buy a small office building containing many small tenants or a strip of stores containing local merchants. If the office space is in demand, it will generate a substantial income whether the tenants are large or small. Likewise, a small strip of stores will be equally profitable if there is traffic and business generated by the neighborhood. It should also be noted that many marginal areas of the City have gone through tremendous change over the years. With the housing shortage, areas which were quiet and somewhat undesirable have now become very much in demand and the rents are skyrocketing. The increase in rents in many of these areas is proportionately greater than the increase in rents in the prime sections of the City.

Money can be made buying real estate anywhere. The important thing is to purchase the real estate in the right location. It does not matter whether it's a fancy neighborhood or a poor one but rather whether the area is stable and attracting businesses and residents. The business areas in many poor areas are extremely busy and the residents are not at liberty to travel to many distant areas in order to make their purchases. These people must buy in their neighborhoods as it is the most convenient and easily accessible to them. A business district surrounded by a large poor population will tend to thrive and succeed.

1

TYPES OF REAL ESTATE INVESTMENTS

There are many different types of real estate investment available to the investor. The spectrum if very broad and runs from the simple to the sophisticated; from the passive to the very active; from the safest to the riskiest; and from those calling for very little money to those requiring substantial sums.

Owning a home

The most common form of real estate investment is that of owning your own home. Not only is it the most common, but it is an investment which has shown a very substantial return. Many people have found that their homes have been their best investments, having increased in value more than other investments and having also been one of the safest and most enjoyable.

Owning a home offers the advantage of giving the purchaser a hedge against inflation because many of the costs of maintaining a home are fixed and will not increase in the future. The mortgage loan obtained from the bank provides for fixed monthly payments and will not increase or change over the life of the loan. As opposed to paying rent, which is not tax-deductible, the homeowner is able to reduce the taxes paid on his ordinary income by the amounts, which he has paid to the bank in interest on the mortgage loan, and also by whatever sum he must pay for annual real estate taxes.

Financing for the purchase of a home is freely available to most buyers. Savings banks and savings and loan associations are primarily intended as sources of funds for home purchases. Banks have traditionally regarded lending on home mortgages as relatively safe; the actual rate of foreclosure is less than 1% of all loans made. Interestingly the major cause of home foreclosures are marital disputes where both parties refuse to make the mortgage payments while they are going through a divorce, and casualty damage, such as fire, to the home where there is insufficient or no insurance coverage to pay the cost of reconstruction. Neither of these are good reasons for losing a home. Spitefulness and gross negligence should always be avoided.

Cooperative or Condominium Ownership

The cooperative or condominium is a form of ownership similar to owing your own home except that you are owing your own apartment in a complex, which is shared with other apartment owners. A cooperative apartment house is an apartment house in which each of the tenants owns his own apartment. The cost of operating the building is divided among the various apartments, and each apartment must pay the maintenance charge proportionate to the apartment's value in relation to the building. All repairs within the apartment are normally the responsibility of the tenant.

When you purchase a cooperative apartment you are really purchasing two things:

(a)   Shares of stock in the cooperative apartment house proportionate to the value of your apartment in relationship to the entire building, and (b) a proprietary lease to the apartment. Normally, the by-laws of the co-op and the lease provide that the shares of stock and proprietary lease must be transferred together. One individual cannot purchase the lease while another purchases the shares of stock.

Condominium ownership serves basically the same purpose as cooperative ownership. In a condominium, the rights of the individual apartment owners are more clearly defined and segregated. Each owner assumes more responsibility for his apartment. A co-op may provide for a blanket mortgage on the entire building, which is paid by each of the tenants through their monthly maintenance charges. In a condominium, there is no mortgage upon the entire building and each owner is responsible for financing his individual apartment. The condominium form of ownership gives greater flexibility to each of the owners, but it may carry the increased cost of financing and of maintenance.

Two-Family Homes and Brownstones

Another fairly common type of ownership found within urban centers is the purchase of two-family homes and brownstones. As the cost of owning a one-family home near the City has substantially increased, many people are seeking to purchase homes where they can rent out part of the building to other tenants for the purpose of defraying their cost of ownership and even to help produce a profit.

The two-family home has always been a common form of ownership. With the increase of the cost of housing, the traditional two-family home is now being constructed as a three family or even four family home. The owner will normally retain an apartment for his own use while renting out the remainder of the house. The income received from the other tenants will pay the owner's mortgage and most of the cost of maintaining the home.

Although the ownership of a home cannot be depreciated, for tax purposes, the owner of a two family home may even deduct from his taxes all expenses incurred in maintaining that portion of his home which is occupied by other tenants.

Brownstones are found primarily near the centers of urban areas. Brownstones range in size from those providing for a single-family residence to those, which have up, to eight or even ten apartments. They are found primarily in the older areas of the City as the majority of them were built more than eighty years ago. The brownstone offers the same advantages as the two family home. However, because of its age, the average purchaser of a brownstone should be prepared to spend substantial sums of money to renovate and modernize the building. A fully renovated brownstone in a good section of the City is very expensive. Brownstones, which sold for $250,000.00 to $750,000.00 on the West side of Manhattan less than ten (10) years ago, are now going for prices ranging from $1,500,000 to $5,000.000.

Land

Land has been a traditional form of investment for those people who are seeking a passive form of investment. There are many different kinds of land, which can be purchased. Land ranges from vacant city lots, to farmland being leased for agricultural purposes, to commercial or industrial land awaiting development. In addition, an investor may purchase the land underneath a large commercial or residential building, which is leased, to the operator and owner of the building. Land, if it is not rented, produces no income and costs money to maintain each year. Although a substantial profit may be realized upon the eventual sale of the land, the investor should take into account the cost of his money, which earns no income, each year that he sits with the land, as well as his cost for taxes, insurance and for maintaining the land.

Small Commercial Buildings

This is a broad areas, which includes small factories, "taxpayers" and loft buildings. A "taxpayer" is a single story building built on a piece of land. Historically, builders while assembling land for development would construct and rent out stores on the property for the purpose of earning sufficient funds to pay their taxes and mortgages. Taxpayers are relatively common within the City and can be found on most streets. As an area in the City develops, the taxpayers may be thrown down so that large buildings can be built on their sites. Taxpayers are almost maintenance free and the problems in operating the building is normally given to the tenant rather than to the landlord.

Loft buildings have served multiple uses throughout the City. Historically, New York was the center for various manufacturers. Until forty years ago, the two largest sources of employment in New York City were the garment industry and the printing trades. To support these industries many small commercial buildings were built. They would range in width from 25 to 100 feet and would be from six to twenty stories tall. On each floor, a different commercial establishment could be found. With new technology and manufacturing procedures, the natures of the garment and printing industries have changed. Rather than being segmented industries with many small manufacturers, they have become fairly unified with large scale manufacturing being the primary motivating force. Small manufacturers are disappearing from the City and these buildings are serving as housing and alternative work centers. Many photographers, fashion designers, computer consultants and service companies are now occupying loft buildings. Space that was once used for manufacturing is now being rented for warehousing and distribution. In addition, loft buildings are now being occupied as places of residence by those individuals who seek large residential space at reasonable prices.

Factory buildings can still be found in many areas near the center of the City or in the outlying districts. These are fairly large sized buildings containing more space for manufacturing. The rent per square foot is more than reasonable and the space is very large. Filling a vacancy may take some time and it is very costly to operate when it is not fully rented. The decline in manufacturing in the City has not helped this situation and good tenants are harder and harder to find.

Apartment Houses

New York City, like all cities, contains many apartment houses of every size, shape, description and kind. There are pre-war (before World War II) apartment houses, walk ups (no elevators), elevator buildings and garden apartments (two-story apartment houses that resemble small houses all attached together), buildings in good areas and buildings in marginal ones. There are apartment houses with tenants who are subject to rent control, rent stabilization, or completely decontrolled (you can charge any rent you wish provided the market will bear it).

In New York City, the ownership of large apartment houses is fairly sophisticated and requires an in-depth knowledge of the operation of various mechanical facilities as well as an understanding of the rent protection laws, which govern the rights of the tenants.

For the rich

I am not going to cover in this book those areas of real estate investment which require substantial sums of money. Needless to say luxury apartment houses, office buildings, industrial centers, hotels and shopping centers are fine investments. But they require substantial sums of money and also a tremendous amount of expertise. These buildings are outside the scope of this book and are not suitable active investments for small or first time investors.

There are many areas in real estate, where the investors can take an almost totally passive role. The investments highlighted above require some activity on the part of the investor. He must get involved with his investments. The investments listed below require almost no activity on the part of the investor. Once the investment is made almost nothing is required of the investor in terms of time.

Mortgages

The mortgage loan is the standard form of financing available for real estate, and it comes in several different forms. Some mortgages are insured by the government under the FHA or similar governmental programs. Mortgages can be purchased in pools, whereby many mortgages are pooled together and then sold as units to a large group of investors. There is safety in numbers and the likelihood of substantial default becomes insignificant when dealing with large numbers of mortgages.

Mortgages can be safe or they can entail a great deal of risk. In general, a mortgage loan is only as good as the building, which secures it, and by the entity promising to pay back the loan. A poor building will produce a risky mortgage loan.

Mortgage loans can be of two kinds: A non-recourse mortgage loan provides that the owner of the mortgage loan will only look for repayment to the property securing the loan and not to the mortgagor, or the person to whom the mortgage loan is being made. A recourse mortgage provides that not only will the mortgagee look to the property to recover his money, but he will also look to the individual or entity that is borrowing the funds. Normally, builders remain personally liable on their mortgage loans, so do purchasers of homes for residential use. As a rule of thumb, if the property is income producing then the lender will not normally require a personal guarantee by the borrower. However, if the property is first being developed, as by a builder, or is being used as the residence of an individual, as a one family home, then the mortgagee will seek the personal guaranty of the borrower.

Numerous mortgages may be placed upon one parcel of real estate. A building may have a first mortgage lien, then a second mortgage lien, and even a third or fourth mortgage lien. Each mortgage is normally subordinate to the previous mortgage. In other words, if a borrower defaults on the first mortgage, then the first mortgagee will have rights, which are superior to that of the second mortgagee. If the second mortgagee wishes to protect his investment, it will also have to make good on the first mortgage or continue to keep its payments current and not in default. Although a second mortgage is considered less secure than a first mortgage, there are many second mortgages, which are far more secure than a first mortgage. It depends upon the nature of each building and the value of the mortgage in relationship to the entire building. A high loan to value (leaving little or no owner's equity in the building) first mortgage on a poorly maintained building in a depressed area will contain a higher degree of risk than a second mortgage on a building with a low first mortgage, plenty of owner's equity, which is well run and in a fine neighborhood.

Net Leased Properties

A common form of investment is the ownership of property which is net leased to another individual or entity. What is a "net lease"? This is a lease in which the person leasing the property assumes all the responsibility for the operation and maintenance of the property and pays a rental to the owner of the property.

There are many different forms and techniques for this form of ownership. A fairly common form is the sales leaseback transaction whereby a highly credit rated quality corporation will sell its building to an investor and then receive a long term lease for the property. The tenant, by doing this, frees its money for other purposes while maintaining the use of the building. The investor, obtains a return on his investment, which is secured by the tenancy of a high quality corporation.

This is commonly found among retail stores and fast food franchises. It may be cheaper for Wal Mart or McDonald's to lease its store rather than own it. This form of transaction was originally referred to as a deed in lieu of a mortgage. The reason for this is that the sales leaseback transaction serves a similar purpose to that of a long-term mortgage loan. There are advantages and disadvantages to a lease as opposed to a mortgage and these will be discussed later on.

A similar form of investment relating to this is the net leased single standing structure. Many post offices are constructed by private individuals and then leased to the United States Government. Many fast food franchise restaurants are built by the franchisor and then sold to private individuals who then lease the restaurant back to the franchisor who in turn leases it to the franchisee who will then operate the restaurant.

Another related area is the ground lease. In order for a builder to obtain maximum leverage upon his property, it is common for the developer of a large office building, which will be leased to a major tenant, to sell the land under the building to an investor and then lease it back. Land is not eligible for depreciation, but the rent paid on the land is tax deductible by the developer. Thus, most office buildings constructed within the part forty years in New York City have been built upon ground leases.

Syndications and Limited Partnerships

For the investor who does not want to go it alone, he has the option of purchasing an interest in a limited partnership or syndication which will own a large piece of real estate or many parcels of real estate throughout the city, the state or the country. Syndications have been set up to purchase all types of property for many different purposes. The limited partnership is frequently used by syndications as it allows the pass through of any tax loss to the partners. It also avoids much of the double taxation to which corporations are subject.

Most syndications in use today were set up for the purpose of obtaining high income tax deductions for those investing. They were commonly called "tax shelters" and flourished in the early 1980s before the tax code was changed to eliminate much of the misuse. More than ninety billion dollars was raised through such tax shelters before the tax law was changed. Most of this money was lost and the tax losses were either disallowed or not usable. Many of these tax shelters were sold as publicly held limited partnerships and a small and scattered secondary market for the units has developed. Some of these partnership units, which originally sold in units of $1,000, became worthless.

Many limited partnerships, however, are truly entities that offer advantages to the investor. They have purchased major office and residential complexes and are operating them efficiently for their investors. They have allowed investors to participate directly in large-scale projects, which normally would not be available to them. Normally, it is difficult to get out once you get in. They are one-way streets and disposing of your interest can be difficult and expensive. You are locked in until the project is sold or liquidated. The advantage is that you get to participate in a large venture, which you would not have been able to do on your own.

Quasi Real Estate Investments

There are many investment areas, which are related to real estate but are operated as separate businesses. Among these areas are parking lots, miniature golf, mobile home parks and building construction. Although they have much to do with real estate, they are not operated in the same manner and fashion. You are actually operating a business, which has real estate as its main asset but you are primarily providing a service. These types of investments are full-time jobs for those individuals involve in their operation and should not be the concern of investors who have other responsibilities.

2

GENERAL CONSIDERATIONS

In making a real estate investment, certain general considerations must be carefully weighted before proceeding. These are applicable to the purchase of almost any type of property and are extremely relevant to the making of any investment. In all probability, many of these considerations have entered into your thinking even if you have not already established formal guidelines.

Each involves three basic factors:

TIME

How much time do you have to devote to the project? Owning real estate is not the same as trading stocks on the internet. You have to see and speak with your tenants, deal with repairmen and service people as well as watch what is happening to your property and the neighborhood in which it is located.

Only you can determine how much time you have. As a rule, things take longer than you think. Also, certain periods require more time than others. If you cannot devote the time required then you will have problems.

MONEY

It is easy to take the plunge but using all your available money on the downpayment leaves none for unexpected repairs or abrupt vacancies. You must have a reserve or back up line of credit. It is much better to err on the conservative side.

Heating systems break in winter and vacancies occur in bad economic times. Expenses will hit you at the worse possible times. You must be prepared or a small set back can ruin what you have tried to build.

RISK

Just as in the stock market, there are many kinds of properties and all kinds of risks. Buying a piece of property with a high mortgage loan (requiring large constant monthly payments) and buying a building which needs many repairs, is in poor condition and has bad tenants, offer possible high future returns but also entails a great deal of risk.

The problem with risk is that its consequences normally arrive at the most unexpected times, Greater risk usually brings greater reward but there is a higher chance of failure. You must be able to live with uncertainty.

Choose something you can live with

It is critically important that the investment you make is in a property that you can handle. If you have an aversion to the investment then, in all probability, it will not be successful. Among the items, which should be taken into consideration, are the time and money required, and the risk involved. If the property demands too much of your time to manage, then it will probably not be a good investment. If you have very little time to devote to your investments, you should consider a very passive investment, which will not require much of your time.

Great consideration should also be given to the amount of money you have available. If you do not have sufficient funds, do not make the investment. Borrowing to your limit puts you under extreme pressure to repay loans. Most investments require time to work themselves out, and if you are under pressure to repay you will not be in a position to wait for a return on the investment. Furthermore, most real estate investments require additional sums of money after the initial investment is made. Very few buildings are purchased in mint condition and there is always a need for additional repairs. Unless you can afford such unanticipated expenditures, you may jeopardize the entire investment.

Also, every investor should weigh the amount of risk that he can afford to accept. Risk determination requires psychological as well as practical considerations. There are many different forms of risk and each should be considered before making an investment. These include loss of money, time and safety. The purchase and management of an apartment house in a low-income neighborhood, for example, may entail a great deal of personal risk to safety.

Liquidity

As opposed to purchasing stock or opening a bank account, real estate generally offers very little liquidity with respect to the sale of an investment. Of course, most property can be readily sold if you want to put in on the auction block at an extremely cheap price. But if you want the proper and fair price for the parcel of real estate you must be prepared to sit and wait for the right buyer to come along. This can be a prolonged process and may take anywhere from a month to a year. Short term investing is only for real estate professionals who are willing to take the risks which are imposed. The average investor must be prepared for the long haul and to sit with his property.

Inflation

Inflation, in general, has been a friend to the real estate investor. It has increased the value of most well situated real estate investments, but it has also increased operational and construction costs. Almost fifty percent of the cost of maintaining the average building, relates to mortgage payments and real estate taxes. These two items have been fairly steady. Once you obtain a mortgage at a fixed rate or within limited variable parameters, you are pretty well assured as to what your monthly mortgage loan payments will be over the life of the mortgage loan. Real estate taxes in New York City have been fairly stable over the past five years. Provided that you do not have excessively long term leases, you will be able to increase your rentals at a greater rate than your operating expenses are increasing.

However, costs have also increased at a greater rate than inflation. The building you purchase could probably not be constructed or renovated five years later for the price paid for the building. This is because construction costs are labor intensive and are of a seasonal nature. They increase at a much greater rate than that of inflation. Interestingly, even the raw materials involved in construction have increased substantially. Lumber and copper, key components, have steadily, although erratically, increased substantially.

Although the Federal Reserve Bank tells us inflation is under control, I am sure everyone has noticed the dramatic increase in heating, electricity and rent which has been caused by the large and rapid increases in crude oil and housing prices.

Strategy

It is critically important that one develop a strategy before proceeding to make any real estate investment. The strategy need not be sophisticated or complex, but can be very simple. The various tactics involved in implementing the strategy can also be worked out at a later time as you are preparing to make the investment.

The main point is to focus on an approach, which will help you achieve your goal. You must be able to live with this approach and be confident that this strategy will work for you. Most successful investors have found a strategy that works for them and simply repeat it again and again as they buy more buildings.

Examples of various successful approaches are as simple as the purchase of a one family home, improving it, selling it, and using the cash received to make a downpayment on a larger more expensive home and then proceeding to improve that home. Another approach might be for the purchase of a building in which you have your store or business. All improvements made in the store or business will benefit the building and you will be there so that you can always see what is going on. Also, as you are in the neighborhood, you can look for fellow tenants to help increase the value of the building and maybe even increase the profitability of your store and business.

A very common strategy being applied in Manhattan, is the purchase of a run-down brownstone in a marginal area, which is on the periphery of a good neighborhood. Many people have purchased brownstones in Chelsea or the Upper West Side and have renovated. Them. Lacking money for hiring contractors, many of these people have become their own and spend their weekends making repairs. As they progress in making the repairs, they also progress in improving their skill and efficiency. As more and more people purchase run down brownstones and renovate them, the marginal areas tend to improve. Although many areas of the City have now been "gentrified" and renovation is proceeding at a rapid pace, there are still many areas available to pioneers. Among the areas available are the Upper East Side from 96th Street to 116th Street, the Lower East Side below 14th Street and the Northern Flatbush Section of Brooklyn.

3

THE BENEFITS OF REAL ESTATE INVESTMENT

Although the ownership of real estate brings certain intangible benefits such as pride of ownership and something to talk about with your friends, there are three primary economic benefits to be derived. These are cash flow, tax savings, and an appreciation in value.

Cash Flow

Cash flow basically is the money you receive on your investment each year. It is not the same as net profit but a different way of calculating return, which is extensively used within the industry. Cash flow refers specifically to all monies you receive during the year on your investment which you are able to keep. For example, the amortization of the principal amount of a mortgage loan (that is, the reduction of the amount which you owe on your loan), would not be included in calculating cash flow. Although repayment of principal on a loan is profit (it reduces your liabilities and increases your capital), as it is not money in your hand, it is not included in calculating cash flow. Likewise, depreciation expense taken on the building you own is not calculated in decreasing the amount of your cash flow. Depreciation is primarily a bookkeeping entry and, as it does not affect the amount of money you receive, it is not included in the calculation of cash flow.

Most other business entities, such as public corporations, calculate their income on the basis of net income received at the end of each year. In calculating its net profit, publicly held corporations will increase its profit by the amount that it has amortized (reduced) its loans, and it will reduce its profit by the amount of depreciation taken on its properties. Net taxable profit is equal to cash flow plus amortization less depreciation.

Most real estate investors, although giving consideration to net taxable profit, rely upon cash flow as their primary means of determining how the property is doing. To the real estate investor, cash flow is equal to net taxable income plus depreciation less amortization expense.

There are good reasons for not giving undue consideration to amortization and depreciation from the point of view of the real estate investor. Most real estate loans are in the form of long-term mortgages upon their properties. These properties, historically, run (have a maturity) for as long as twenty or thirty years. The average investor is not that concerned in the reduction of a mortgage loan, which would not come due for another twenty-five years. All the investor is concerned with is the making of the monthly payments required by the terms of the mortgage loan agreement. There is no question that the amortization of a loan is beneficial to the real estate investor as it reduces his liabilities and allows him a chance to refinance the property sooner. In the event the property is sold, the lower the mortgage loan, the higher the cash he would normally receive. Amortization, however, is regarded as having secondary significance and the primary concern is given to the cash received each year. Many consider amortization to be detrimental. Although they can deduct the interest portion of their mortgage from their tax returns, amortization is nor a tax-deductible item.

Likewise, depreciation also has very little consequence to the average investor. Depreciation is the method for calculating the wear and tear suffered by an asset used in a business. For example, a manufacturer who purchases a machine for $50,000, which has an average useful life of five years, would depreciate the value of this machine by $10,000 a year. At the end of five years, he would have depreciated the machine by $50,000 and he would then have to purchase a new machine.

This is also true in real estate to the extent that many of the mechanical systems in a building age over time and need to be replaced. Inflation, however, has been a great friend of the real estate investor and although the building, which the investor might own, has become older, it has not declined in value. For that matter, an average building, in a good location, has substantially increased in value overt time. It is for this reason that the typical real estate investor pays little concern to depreciation when calculating his income. He prefers to rely on cash flow, or actual cash received, if repairs have to be made to the building because of its age. Such repairs will be deducted from the cash flow for the year in which the repairs are to be made.

Tax Savings

Another advantage accruing to the owner of real estate is that he may obtain substantial tax savings while sitting on his investment. Although raw land may not be depreciated, almost everything else can. For instance, investor may purchase a building for $100,000 and depreciate the building the following twenty years, in round numbers, each year he will deduct from his taxable income $5,000 and allocate this to depreciation. The Internal Revenue Service allows everyone to depreciate buildings or equipment on the theory that as they become older their economic use declines and dissipates. This is also true with respect to buildings. If a building is held long enough, it will become totally "worthless". However, with the advent of moderate inflation, buildings have not declined but increased in value. Although the investor could take $5,000 a year as a depreciation expense, and deduct that expense from the income from the building, thereby reducing taxable income therefore, it is primarily a bookkeeping entry and, in all probability, assuming a stable market, the building has in reality not declined by $5,000 even though it is a tax deductible item. This amount can also be greatly increased, if the investor were to take a mortgage loan on the property. Going back to the above example, if the investor had purchased the property for $100,000 and borrowed $75,000 as a mortgage loan on the property, he would still be entitled to the same $5,000 annually as depreciation. Rather than depreciating 5% annually on his investment, he would now be depreciating 20% annually or $5,000 on his $25,000 investment.

Appreciation of Investment

Over the years, well situated real estate can substantially increase in value. The old maxim is true. The three most important things in real estate are location, location and location. Besides the annual cash flow, which the investor receives on his real estate, and besides tax savings, which may reduce his taxes, there is also the chance for a substantial appreciation in the investment. Everyone has heard stories about someone who purchased a brownstone on the West Side, or in Chelsea, or in Brooklyn Heights, that has multiplied in value over the years. However, not many people talk about their investments in other areas, which have declined and become almost totally worthless.

With any investment, risks are taken and there is no guarantee that it will appreciate in value. The investor owning appreciated property may continue to retain the property, or may enter into a tax free exchange of his property for another property, or may sell the property to a third party. Upon the sale of the property, the investor, provided that he is not a regular dealer in real estate, will obtain capital gains treatment upon the sale. Rather than being taxed as it was ordinary income, the gain upon the sale of the property will be taxed at a substantially reduced rate.

Although the above three benefits from investing in real estate, cash flow, tax savings and capital gains can be obtained separately from other forms of investment, it is rare to find them together, in a single investment. An individual may purchase rare art with the hope of appreciation but will not receive any cash flow or tax savings while owning this investment. Likewise, many individuals invest in so-called tax shelters (which caused substantial damage) offering very little cash flow, almost rarely any capital gains and at best, dubious tax savings. The investor may lose his investments and his "tax shelter" may be set aside by the Internal Revenue Service. He can suffer the worse of two possible outcomes, the loss of his money and paying taxes on income he never receives. Someone may purchase bonds or fixed income investments for the purpose of obtaining steady cash flow each year but it is rare for such an investor to obtain tax savings or capital gains from this investment. Although municipal bonds offer tax savings, the investor must sacrifice and accept a reduced interest rate to obtain these tax savings. Likewise, bonds and fixed income investments have not had a friend in inflation and although you receive your principal when the bond matures, it is not worth the same amount as the funds you originally invested.

Real estate is a far superior investment than common stocks. Although common stocks offer liquidity, in the sense that you can buy and sell your investment at almost anytime, there are many other advantages which favor real estate over common stocks.

Investors in common stock purchase either shares of companies, which pay high dividends with very little future growth, or those paying small current dividends but are exhibiting a rapid growth of earnings. It is very rare that an individual will find a stock which offers both high yield and high appreciation. With real estate, it is possible to make an investment which offers both a high current return with the chance for a substantial increase in value over the life of the investment. With the purchase of stock, the only form of borrowing available is that of opening a margin account. With a margin account, you are subject to paying a rate of interest, which will fluctuate from month to month. The amount of money, which you can borrow upon any stock, is limited by the margin requirements as periodically established by the Federal Reserve Bank and your broker. If the stock declines in value, even if you have the money to pay for the interest on the margin account, you will have to put up additional money to reduce the amount of your loan from the brokerage firm. With real estate, it is possible to obtain long-term mortgage loans at fixed rates of interest. Your interest payments will not fluctuate from month to month but will remain constant over the life of the loan. Once you know what your regular monthly mortgage payments will be, you can project your cash needs more accurately in relation to your investment. Furthermore, the sources of mortgage loans are more varied than those of loans on stock. You may obtain a mortgage loan from any of a number of financial institutions, friends, close relatives, and even the seller of the property. It is very common for a seller to give the purchaser a mortgage for part of the purchase price in order to induce a purchaser to but a piece of real estate when he does not have all the money necessary for the purchase and these interest rates are negotiable. Mortgage loans, once obtained are not usually tied to the value of the investment. If real estate goes up or down in value, you still have the same loan, provided that you are able to meet the monthly payments.

Very few common stocks offer any tax saving advantages. Although a few utilities offer partially tax free dividends, these dividends are deemed to be a return on capital and reduce your basis in the stock. There are many more tax savings available to the real estate investor than the purchaser of common stock. In general, those who buy common stock receive a lower return because of taxes. Almost all dividends received by investors are subject to double taxation. The corporation, in which he owns stock, must pay taxes on all income received. As dividends are paid from the net income earned by the corporation, the corporation must pay taxes on its income before it can allocate a portion of its income as a dividend to its investors. When the investor receives this dividend, he will then pay personal income taxes upon the dividend received. Real estate may be purchased by individuals, partnerships, limited liability companies and subchapter S corporations and can thereby avoid double taxation.

The stock markets' performance over the past few years has been exceptional. The market has outperformed everything. We can only wait and see if this remarkable performance continues or whether it will lead to disaster. Many sectors of the stock market have already produced "roller coaster" effects for their shareholders.

4

MORTGAGES

Very few people purchase real estate for all cash. Most obtain mortgages to enable them to buy the property. The type, kind, amount and interest rate paid upon the mortgage loan is very critical in determining the economics of the investment. Most real estate mortgage loans substantially exceed the amount of money actually invested in the property. Because mortgages are so important to real estate investing, may types and varieties have developed. All mortgage payments can be divided into two portions. One is the interest payment due on the amount borrowed while the other portion represents a payment and reduction of the amount of the loan. The portion of the mortgage paid in reduction of the loan is called amortization. As was said previously, the interest on the loan is deductible from your taxes while the amortization portion is not. If there is no amortization of the mortgage loan, then the mortgage loan will be due in full, on the date it matures and comes due.

The Mortgage Constant and Amortization

The mortgage constant is the combination of the interest and amortization portions of the mortgage loan. For example, if your have a $100,000 mortgage loan bearing interest at 7% per annum and you pay the bank $8,000 during the first year, then:

A. $7,000 is the interest component of your mortgage payment which is 7%,

B. $1,000 is your amortization component of your mortgage payment which is 1%, and

C. $8,000 is your mortgage constant for a total of 8%.

As will be seen, the mortgage constant will remain at $8,000 but with the passing of time, the interest component will decrease and the amortization portion will increase. As you make amortization payments, the principal amount of the loan will decrease and therefore the interest component, which is in this case 7% of the principal amount of the loan, will decrease. The mortgage constant payment will remain at $8,000 but the percent applied to the loan principal will increase. When the loan has been reduced to $80,000, your mortgage constant will be 10% ($8000/$80,000) of the principal amount of the loan.

The average investor is concerned with keeping the mortgage constant as low as possible. The monthly payments for interest and amortization should be as low as possible. The lower the mortgage constant the higher the cash flow on the property. If the mortgage constant is too high, it will substantially reduce the cash flow on the investment. Both the interest and amortization portions of the mortgage loan can be negotiated. With respect to the interest portion, the sole area of negotiation is the rate of interest being charged on the mortgage loan. The higher the interest rate, the higher the interest portion of the mortgage payment will be. In general, mortgage payments are made monthly, quarterly or on an annual basis. A monthly mortgage payment is the most common, as the mortgagor (the borrower) need not make a very large payment as would be required with an annual payment. Almost all one family mortgages require monthly payments. Quarterly payments (a payment once every three months) may be found with commercial and multiple dwelling mortgage loans.

With the amortization portion of the mortgage payment, there is also room for negotiation. Most investors seek to keep the amortization portion as low as possible so that they increase their immediate cash flow.

The most common form of amortization schedule is that which is geared to self-amortize the mortgage over its life. One family homes traditionally carry self-amortizing mortgage schedules. The mortgagor makes a constant monthly payment towards the interest and amortization, which is geared to amortize the mortgage loan over its life, When the mortgagor makes his last payment, it will normally be sufficient to have paid off the entire mortgage loan with any accrued interest. The longer the mortgage loan is, the smaller the monthly payments. A fifteen-year mortgage loan will require larger monthly payments than a twenty-five year mortgage loan of the same amount and with the same interest rate. It should be noted that although the monthly payments will be smaller, the total amount of interest payments over the life of the loan will be greater.

Many investment properties do not have self-amortizing mortgages. There are several reasons for this. The mortgage may have been given by the seller to induce the purchaser to purchase the property and the seller does not wish to give a mortgage loan for a long period of time. The seller would rather give a ten-year mortgage than a twenty-five year mortgage. However, the property does not produce sufficient cash flow to amortize the full amount of the loan over ten years, but requires twenty-five years to do so. The parties may then agree to a ten-year mortgage amortized over a twenty-five year payment schedule. This means that at the end of ten years there will be a remaining balance due on the mortgage loan. This remaining balance is commonly called a "balloon". At the end of ten years, the mortgagor will have to find the necessary funds to pay off the mortgage. At that time the mortgagor may seek to refinance the property with another mortgagee or may enter into a new agreement with the existing mortgagee to extend the mortgage over a longer period of time at different terms. If the mortgage is payable as interest only, without amortization, it is commonly called a "standing" or "bullet" mortgage as the principal balance remains standing at the same level throughout the life of the mortgage and is all due at once, at the end of the loan period.

The Nature of the Mortgage Loan

A mortgage loan normally consists of two documents. One is the note or bond, which represents the promise to pay the amount due on the loan with the required rate of interest and terms. This note or bond may be with recourse or non-recourse. A recourse loan means that the lender will look solely to the property to recover its investment, it will not seek to hold the borrower personally liable. This is generally a matter of negotiation. Traditionally, all owners of non-income producing property are required to sign recourse notes to obtain mortgage loans. Almost all one-family mortgage notes have provided that the signer of the mortgage note is liable in the event he defaults and fails to make his payments. Builders also, traditionally, remain liable on mortgage notes and must sign personally.

The second portion of the mortgage documentation is the mortgage itself, which provides for the security of the loan. Bear in mind that a mortgage is a lien, which becomes an obligation upon the property. The mortgage is normally recorded with the City Registrar or County Clerk. In the event the mortgage loan is not repaid, the mortgagee (lender) may foreclose upon the property and sell the property at public auction to recover the amount due on the loan.

A mortgage loan may be collateralized with mortgages on several properties owned by the same mortgagor. (This is called a "spreader" agreement.) The mortgage may provide that the mortgage loan will be due and payable upon sale of the property, or upon failure of the mortgagor to pay real estate taxes, or failure to maintain the property in good condition.

Kinds of Mortgage Loans

There are many different mortgage loans. Up to now we have spoken about first mortgages; that is, a mortgage, which is a first lien upon the property. Many investors have second and third mortgages upon the properties, which they own, these additional mortgages are subordinate or subject to the first mortgage. A second mortgagee seeking to foreclose on property where the mortgagor failed to make payments, must make all payments on the first mortgage, which has a priority over his mortgage. Also, if the first mortgagee commences foreclosure proceedings because of the mortgagor's failure to pay, then the second mortgagee will have to arrange to satisfy the first mortgagee if he is to retain his investment.

Mortgages are also granted on leases as well as on the actual real estate. This is called a "leasehold mortgage" and is very commonly found with large office buildings where the land is owned by someone else and is leased to the developer. The developer may have a long-term lease on the land in order to construct a large office building upon the property. In this case the leasehold mortgage is secured by the lease. If the mortgagor fails to make the payments, then the mortgagee may foreclose and take possession of the building on the property subject to the lease. These ground leases are normally made for tax purposes as land is not depreciable while lease payments are deductible as a taxable expense. Leasehold mortgages are also found on garages and other operating entities where the owner of the garage or entity leases the property from an investor who operates a business upon the property. The mortgage is secured by the lease and by the business.

In general, first mortgages upon land and buildings are normally the safest for investors such as banks and insurance companies to own. A second mortgage or leasehold mortgage normally contains a higher grade of risk and therefore the mortgagee is entitled to a higher rate of interest. It should be noted however, that a second mortgage upon a piece of property having a very small first mortgage may be safer than a large first mortgage upon a poor piece of property.

Refinancing the Mortgage

It is very common for an investor to refinance a mortgage, once his mortgage has been paid or when it has been reduced to a very low level. If the investor obtains more money from a lending institution on his property, he gets to keep this money, and it is considered to be a non-taxable transaction, many investors, rather than selling a property will refinance it when the mortgage is reduced. Each time they refinance the mortgage, they get a large sum of money, which although not as large as the sum of money they would get on a sale, it still a considerable amount and it is not subject to taxation.

Another form of refinancing is called "recasting" a mortgage. This occurs when the monthly payments being made by the mortgagor are relatively high with respect to the remaining balance of the mortgage. The mortgagor may then go to the mortgagee and agree to reduce the mortgage payments so that they will bear the same proportion to the loan as they did originally. For example, an investor may obtain a new mortgage from a lending institution requiring monthly mortgage payments of 10% per annum with initially 2% being applied to amortization. The mortgagor will obtain a $100,000 mortgage by agreeing to pay $1,000 monthly for interest and amortization. Of the $12,000 being paid annually on the mortgage loan, $10,000 will be allocated to interest and $2,000 to amortization of principal. As time passes, the mortgage will have been reduced to $50,000 with the investor still paying the same $1,000 monthly. However, at the $50,000 level, on an annual basis, only $5,000 is being applied to interest (10% of $50,000 is $5,000) and the balance of $7,000 is being applied to amortization of principal. Originally, the mortgagor was only paying $2,000 a year in amortization, but as the loan matures, he is now paying $7,000 annually in amortization. The borrower may speak with the lending institution and they may agree to reduce the amortization portion of the loan to $1,000, which is the equivalent of 2% of the remaining $50,000 of the mortgage loan balance. The investor will now be paying $500 monthly in mortgage payments or $6,000 annually, which is being allocated as $5,000 to interest and $1,000 to amortization. This $6,000 a year reduction in his mortgage payments will act a to increase his cash flow by $6,000 annually. Again, this is a tax-free transaction and the investor pays no tax for increasing his cash flow.

With declining interest rates, many borrowers are refinancing their mortgage loans simply to take advantage of lower rates. When rates are very high and rising everyone wants fixed rate loans, which carry the same interest rate throughout the life of the loan. Only then do many people shift to variable rate loans, which are adjusted every month, year or five years, so that they automatically get the advantage of lower rates.

Consolidation and Wraparound Mortgages

When making a sale of a piece of property, many investors are required to take back, as part of the consideration for the sale, a second, or junior mortgage, to help finance the transaction for the purchaser, who does not have sufficient cash to purchase the building. This is called a "purchase money" mortgage loan. In many instances, if the seller does not agree to give the purchase money second mortgage loan to the buyer, then the buyer will not purchase the building. Another alternative occurs when the first mortgage has been substantially paid down and the investor wishes to obtain additional financing on his building so that he can free up some cash to make another investment. There are various alternatives to taking a junior mortgage.

The two main approaches are consolidation with the existing mortgage loans or wrapping the subordinate mortgage around the existing mortgages. We will examine both approaches and show how they have developed.

The classic example of a consolidated mortgage occurs when an individual has substantially paid down the existing first mortgage and the lender or mortgagee is prepared to lend additional money to the mortgagor upon his property. The mortgagee might simply lend the additional money and take an additional mortgage on the property. For example, if a mortgage of $50,000 was originally given on a parcel and the loan has now been paid down to $30,000, the mortgagee might be prepared to lend the mortgagor an additional $30,000 bringing the total loan on the property to $60,000. The mortgagee might feel that the property has substantially appreciated in value and that its loan of $60,000 is fully secured by the value of the property. The lender could give a second mortgage loan and then hold both a first and second mortgage on the property.

Rather than do the above, the mortgagee will give a second mortgage but will then enter into a consolidation and extension agreement with the borrower whereby both mortgages will be considered as if they are one mortgage loan. Instead of making two separate periodic payments on two mortgages, the mortgagor will make one payment on a single consolidated mortgage. Any default by the mortgagor will be a default upon the entire amount borrowed. Many lending institutions are prohibited from giving second mortgage loans and this is a method of avoiding the problem.

A borrower may approach a lender and ask for an additional loan upon his property. Rather than being in the position of a second mortgagor, the lender may agree to purchase the existing first mortgage from the previous lender by means of an assignment of the mortgage. The new lender will then consolidate this assignment of mortgage with the new mortgage received as security for the new loan and become the holder of a consolidated first mortgage rather than a second mortgage. Many lenders, quite rightly feel more secure with a consolidated first mortgage than with a second mortgage even if the amount of the loan under the consolidated first mortgage is the same amount as the total of the first and second mortgage, because, all being equal, a first mortgage offers a greater security to the mortgagee than a second mortgage.

A more sophisticated approach is for the second mortgagee to make the loan and to assume that responsibility for making the first mortgage payments. The mortgagor would make one payment to the second mortgagee and the second mortgagee would use part of the payment for paying the first mortgage. This can be done through an escrow provision contained in the second mortgage. It can also be done by the second mortgagee taking a mortgage, which includes the amount, due on the first mortgage with his second mortgage encompassing the first mortgage or "wrapping around" it.

With a wrap-around mortgage, the mortgagor has only one mortgage to pay. The holder of the wrap-around mortgage assumes the duty of paying the underlying first mortgage with part of the payments it received on its wrap-around mortgage. The mortgagee is in full control of the mortgage underlying its wrap around mortgage.

Wrap-around mortgages are flexible devices and serve numerous purposes. A seller may own a parcel subject to an existing mortgage loan bearing interest at the rate of 6% per annum in an environment when loans are going for 12%. Rather than pass the benefits of this cheap mortgage on the purchaser, it may make the sale subject to a wrap around mortgage bearing interest at 12%. The seller will receive 12% interest on his purchase money wrap around mortgage and will only have to pay 6% on the underlying mortgage, thereby earning the 6% differential.

In another approach, the underlying mortgage may bear interest at the rate of 8% per annum and with amortization at 4% per annum. The wrap-around mortgage may provide for interest-only payments of 12% per annum so that the holder of the mortgage, although not receiving additional cash, will be amortizing his underlying mortgage while maintaining the value of his wrap-around mortgage. The mortgage he holds will remain the same and he will be owed the same sum of money. His mortgage loan will be continually reduced and he will owe less money. His equity in the wrap-around mortgage (the difference between what he is owed and what he owes) will increase.

A wrap around mortgage may be for any sum of money, larger than or equal to the underlying mortgage. It may be for a term of years equal to or substantially longer than the underlying mortgage. It may bear interest or require amortization at rates substantially different from the underlying mortgage. There may be one or many underlying mortgages, which are wrapped around the mortgage. Wrap around mortgages are extremely flexible and their uses are only limited by the creativity of the parties involved in the transaction.

5

DEPRECIATION

Depreciation offers the primary source of tax benefits to investors in real estate. Depreciation allows investors to record a theoretical decline in value in their property each year and deduct this theoretical decline in value from their taxable income. Depreciation today is primarily a bookkeeping entry and does not reflect reality. It does not require the expenditure of cash and has the sole effect of reducing the investor's income taxes.

The Nature of Depreciation

Depreciation is a method intended to compensate any investor or businessman for the decline in usefulness of any machinery or other equipment used in manufacturing or business. If a manufacturer purchases a piece of equipment for $100,000 and it has a useful life of five years, then the manufacturer would have to set aside $20,000 annually, if he were to have $100,000 available at the end of five years to replace the existing equipment which is no longer useful in his trade and business. To compensate the businessman for the decline in usefulness of his equipment, he would be allowed to depreciate his equipment by $20,000 annually for tax purposes. The Internal Revenue Code allows the businessman to deduct $20,000 annually from his income as representing the cost of the decline in the usefulness of the equipment.

For the manufacturer, the decline in use of his equipment, is a real expense although it only requires the expenditure of cash initially upon the purchase of the equipment. The manufacturer may purchase a new piece of equipment when the existing equipment wears out. Had the manufacturer taken the purchase of the equipment as an expense when he purchased it (which is allowed for smaller items), he would have reduced his income in the year of purchase by $100,000 and taken no further expenses over the life of the equipment until he needed to replace it with a new piece of equipment.

The Internal revenue Service considers this to be a distortion of income as the expense for the equipment is not actually realized in the year of purchase but is spread out over its five-year useful life.

This same principal applies to the purchase of a building. No building was built to stand forever, and as each year passes, the building begins to show signs of deterioration. The mechanical systems in the building will begin to show signs of deterioration faster than the actual structure. As time passes, the heating system, plumbing and elevators will need to be repaired or replaced, roofs begin to leak, and cracks develop within cement walls. The Internal Revenue Code allows the real estate investor to be compensated for this deterioration by allocating a certain portion of income each year toward depreciation of the building. The amounts allowed have been changed by the Internal Revenue Code over time and the amounts allowed also depend upon the class of structure. Different types of buildings, such as apartment houses, office buildings and industrial warehouses, have different rates of depreciation allocated to them by the Internal Revenue Service.

Depreciation and Inflation

Inflation whether it is at 10% per annum or 3% has had a profound effect on the concept of depreciation. Inflation has caused the manufacturer to take a smaller amount of depreciation than necessary to replace his equipment and has caused the real estate investor to take a greater rate of depreciation than the value of his building has actually decline.

With respect to the manufacturer, even if he saves the $20,000 a year which he is taking in depreciation to purchase a new piece of equipment for the same price that he paid for it five years ago. If he paid $100,000 for the equipment five years ago, his cost of replacement may be $120,000 or even $50,000. Unfortunately the Internal Revenue Code only allows the manufacturer to set up a depreciation reserve of $100,000, which is equivalent to the original purchase price of the equipment. The manufacturer will have to find the additional $20,000 or $50,000, which he needs for the purchase of the replacement equipment from another source. Inflation has not treated the manufacturer fairly and has penalized him for the increased cost of his equipment.

Inflation, however, has been more than kind to the real estate investor. Rather than the building owned by the investor declining in value with age, the average building has tended in increase in value. This is because the same building can no longer be constructed for the same price, which the investor paid for it. Market fluctuation has a much greater affect upon the value of the building than the factor of the building's age. Furthermore, a building in good condition, is worth substantially more than a newer building in poor condition. All that the depreciation expense does is give the investor a tax benefit, which he can use to offset against the income received from the building.

Depreciation and Tax Basis

The depreciation expense taken each year by the real estate investor reduces his basis of cost for the purchase of the building for tax benefits. If an investor purchased a building for $100,000 and takes a depreciation expense of $2,000 during the first year of ownership, then his cost price of the building for tax purposes becomes $98,000. If he continues to take $2,000 of the depreciation expense during the second year, then his cost basis of the building, for tax purposes, will be further reduced to $96,000. This reduction of tax cost basis will continue each year until the cost basis for tax purposes finally is zero. At that point in time, the investor will no longer be entitled to take any depreciation expense against his income. For the average real estate investor, who is not a dealer in real estate, the difference between the price at which the property is sold and what his tax cost basis is becomes his taxable gain upon the sale of the property. This gain will normally be treated as a capital gain and be taxed at a lower tax rate than ordinary income.

Land and Depreciation

In general, an investor may not take depreciation on the cost of land. This is because land does not have a useful life but is there forever, or so we hope. If improvements have been made to the land, then the investor will be allowed to depreciate them. For example, if an investor constructs a garden near his building, he would be allowed to depreciate the cost of setting up the garden over its useful life. It is for this reason that when most real estate investors are purchasing land and the building constructed on the land, they attempt to allocate as little as possible to the cost of the land. They can depreciate the building for tax purposes but they cannot depreciate that portion of the cost allocated to the value of the land.

Useful Life–vs–Economic Life

Normally, the useful life of any building should correspond to its economic life. When a building is no longer useful, it should have no economic value. Likewise, a building should continue to have economic value while it has a useful life. However, in reality, this is not always the case. An investor buying a recently constructed building in a declining neighborhood may find that the building still has a long and useful life, but because of the nature of the neighborhood, the building has a very limited economic promise. Similarly, an investor may purchase a bowling alley in a neighborhood where there are too many bowling alleys and the bowling alley purchased by the investor is not economically viable. In such circumstances, the economic life of the property is much shorter than the useful life of the property and will not properly reflect the depreciation expense being taken.

Mortgages and Depreciation

An investor is allowed to take depreciation upon the total cost of his investment regardless of how much he paid in cash for the building and how much came from a mortgage loan. Let us say that two investors purchased two different buildings for $100,000 each and with each allocating $10,000 towards the land, it makes no differences that one investor purchased the property for all cash while the other investor obtained a $50,000 mortgage loan toward the purchase price. They would both be allowed to calculate depreciation on the respective buildings on a cost basis of $90,000. The investor who paid the full $100,000 cash for the property would be allowed to take a depreciation expense of $4,500 a year on a straight line basis of 20 years ($4,500 for 20 years which is $90,000) while the investor who only put up $50,000 would be entitled to the same $4,500 depreciation rate on straight line basis. Obviously, the investor who paid less cash for the property would be entitled to take a greater percentage of depreciation in relationship to his cash investment. This approach, which is referred to as leveraging an investment, can have both benefits and detriments.

WHAT IS A TAX SHELTER?

In general, a tax shelter is a device which will postpone or reduce income taxes that an individual would normally have to pay. As generally used, a tax shelter will reduce an individual's taxable income for a given year.

It should be noted, that this elimination of taxable income is rarely forever as the individual will one day have to pay the taxes which are due and owing. Tax shelters can postpone the realization of a tax liability or they can convert a tax liability, which would be taxed as ordinary income, into a liability which may be taxed at the lower capital gains rate. Real estate investment can both postpone the payment of income taxes and convert ordinary income into long-term capital gains.

Because of the massive abuse of tax shelters from the late 1970s to the mid 1980s, the Tax Reform Act of 1986 sharply curtailed the use of tax shelters and did substantial damage to the real estate industry. Most losses generated by real estate are now deemed to be passive losses and may be used to offset passive losses but not by passive losses. Also in conjunction with these reforms, the methods of depreciation were radically changed. Needless to say, a full discussion of this subject is beyond the scope of this book. Information on current tax laws is readily available and much has been published on this subject which is easy to understand.

Depreciation and Amortization

As we said above, depreciation, once the property is purchased, is merely a book-keeping entry, which reduces a taxable income from the property. There is no cash outlay for depreciation and it is only a method for reducing taxable income. Depreciation expense has no effect upon cash flow.

Amortization is not a tax-deductible expense and requires an expenditure of cash by the investor. Amortization reduces the investor's liabilities on the property but does not affect the investor's tax liabilities.

Let us assume that an individual purchased a property which has a zero cash flow. If the depreciation expense exceeded the amortization portion of his mortgage constant (the constant is interest and amortization), then the property would have a tax loss but would not have negative cash flow. The investor would not be realizing any cash flow on the property nor would he be expending any money to maintain the property, but he would show a loss for tax purposes. Whether he could utilize this loss under the present tax laws would depend on whether he had passive income and the nature of his current income. In the above hypothetical example, if amortization exceeded depreciation, then the investor would be showing taxable income even though he was not receiving any cash from the property. This is commonly called "phantom income".

With respect to the average mortgage loan, especially those loans that are self-amortizing, the rate of amortization increases as the loan matures. In the early stages of the life of the mortgage loan, the investor's mortgage payments consist primarily of interest, with very little being applied towards amortization. As time progresses and the principal amount of the mortgage slowly declines, providing that the mortgage constant remains the same, the portion of the mortgage payment allocated to amortization will greatly increase until it surpasses the interest portion. Assuming that the investor is taking a straight-line method of depreciation, his tax benefits relating to cash flow will gradually decrease. Let us remember that taxable income is equal to cash flow plus amortization less depreciation. As amortization increases, the investor's taxable income will also increase. This is especially applicable where the cash flow remains constant throughout the life of the mortgage loan, as is the case with net leased properties.

The Cross Over Point

Real estate investors refer to that exact moment in time where the amortization portion of the mortgage payment exceeds the depreciation expense as the "cross over point". It is at that instant when the investment losses its tax benefits and begins to incur tax liabilities. If the investor continues to hold the property after the cross over point, then he can incur greater taxable income than the actual cash flow from the property. This is not a reason to sell the property, provided that you are satisfied with it, but it is worth considering.

Depreciation and Capital Gains

Let us return to the investor who elected to take a straight-line method depreciation on the property. Assuming that the investor purchased the property for $100,000 and allocated $10,000 to land and $90,000 to the building. Suppose the building is being depreciated over twenty years, which would produce a depreciation expense of $4,500 annually. If the investor, after the first year, sold the property for the same price he had paid for it, namely $100,000 he would realize a capital gain of $4,500. This is because the depreciation expense reduces the investor's tax basis in the property each year. After the first year, the investor's tax basis will be reduced by $4,500 to $95,500. After the second year, it will be reduced to $91,000 ($100,000 minus $4,500 and $4,500). The investor will be entitled to continue to depreciate the building until he has accumulated $90,000 of depreciation expense, which is his original allocation of the purchase price to the building. At that time, twenty years later, his tax basis in the building would be zero, but his tax basis in the building would still be $10,000 as he never took depreciation on the land. If the investor after twenty years sold the land and building for the same price he paid for it, he would realize a capital gain of $90,000.

Capital Gains and the Dealer

A dealer is defined for tax purposes as an individual whose normal trade and business is dealing in real estate. This is not someone who operates real estate for a livelihood but rather someone who earns his income by buying and selling real estate, converting buildings to cooperative or condominium ownership, or subdividing lots for resale. If the ownership of real estate is not considered an investment by the individual but rather a form of inventory, he will not be entitled to capital gains treatment on the sale. Any sale of real property by an individual who is deemed to be a dealer will result in ordinary income and loss. This is the equivalent of a diamond merchant who buys and sells his diamonds in his usual trade and business. He incurs ordinary gains and losses upon each transaction. An individual who buys a diamond for investment and later sells it for a gain, will be entitled to a capital gain.

6

DISTRESSED PROPERTY

Many individuals interested in purchasing real estate for the first time usually inquire as to how to do so with little or no cash. They are willing to work hard but have little money.

In New York City, the only way to buy property for little or no cash is to purchase property in poor and depressed areas. The buildings that cater to these areas are generally marginal. The expenses of operating the building may equal or exceed the income presently generated from the rents being collected from the tenants in the building. The person purchasing such properties will have to take very tight control of the expenses of the building while attempting to increase the rent roll, and struggling to collect the existing rents which the tenants are required to pay. These buildings can be purchased cheaply and with little cash because that is reflected in their real economic value.

No matter how nice a building is, if it is operating at a loss, it is not worth the value of the bricks and mortar and that went into its construction. These buildings may also be dangerous to operate in that they are located in bad areas with high crime rates. As the property does not produce enough income to be properly operated and maintained, the tenants will be dissatisfied with the services being provided by the landlord. In conjunction with all of the above, a poorly maintained building attracts only bad tenants thereby making rents even more difficult to collect. In many instances the Landlord & Tenant Part of the Civil Court acts as the dispute resolution center, providing landlords with the means of collecting rent and the tenants with a forum for formally expressing their grievances. Both sides are normally dissatisfied with the Court system as it is overly crowded and inadequately staffed. The Landlord & Tenant Part of the Civil Court acts more as a dispute resolution center and conciliation facility than as a Court of Justice.

The tenancy in these buildings normally consists of poor people who have trouble meeting their rental payments. Therefore, the rent is always late and the landlord must continually remind the tenants to pay it. In addition, there has been substantially deferred maintenance. Rather than making the usual repairs to preserve the property, the prior landlords have in all probability stopped making any necessary repairs and much of the equipment and systems, which should have been in proper working order, are now in a state of disrepair. If the previous landlord had taken decent care of the building, then it would just require the regular maintenance. As the previous landlords neglected these systems and equipment, they now require extensive repairs to restore them to proper operating order. Because many of these buildings are very old, there is a continual need for substantial repairs and the income from which to derive the money to make these repairs is not always available.

Winters are very harsh to these buildings as fuel is a major factor and 80% of fuel costs are incurred from December through March of each year. Fuel costs may equal anywhere from 15% to even 30% of the total operating costs of these buildings. This major expense is not spread out over the entire year and the bulk of this expense is incurred in just three months. This problem is further aggravated by insufficient and antiquated fuel systems, lack of building insulation and drafty windows. Installing new windows or a new heating system, let alone providing proper insulation, are very costly endeavors. Many of these buildings do not generate sufficient cash flow during the winter to pay all the fuel bills. It is a tremendous struggle for landlords in poor areas to survive the winter months.

It should also be noted that many depressed and poor areas get worse rather than better. It is nice to believe that everything will improve with time, but that is not always the case. Bad areas in the New York City have tended to get worse or at best, remain unchanged, but not to improve with the passing of time. Those areas that do get better are the exceptions to the rule. As each group of people living within the area achieve some economic improvement, they tend to move to better areas, which offer more decent housing. The apartments they occupied are then rented by individuals coming from a lower economic class.

At present, we are experiencing a real estate boom. Prices all over have increased dramatically. Areas which people were fearful of have now come into demand. This is all part of the cycle. Better to buy property when no one else is interested than to fight with others to buy junk.

Distressed property must be priced in recognition of its condition. It is not wise to pay top dollar for bad property in the belief that it is still cheaper than good property. To make any sense, bad property must be substantially cheaper than good property. You must but this property for its true value and pay a substantial premium for the "Hype."

Positive Aspects of Distressed Property

The government has recognized the needs of the urban poor and has pumped millions of dollars into urban areas under different programs. Both the Federal and local government are trying to preserve distressed areas. Many of the rents are now being subsidized by the government so that the tenants can afford to have decent housing. There are many programs to encourage individuals to renovate and improve the existing housing stock.

Many buildings in distressed areas are not earning any income because they have been neglected by their owners and not properly maintained. A conscientious owner who devotes time to his buildings may be able to earn a decent return if he closely watches his expenses and income. Many of the present owners of these owners are absentee owners who are not there to see exactly how the building is operating or to deal effectively with their tenants. A conscientious owner can turn around a building, which is losing money, and make it profitable but this will require much aggravation as well as time.

Labor–vs–Capital

As has been noted by all economists, including Karl Marx, there is a trade off between capital and labor, which affects the means and costs of production. Basically, labor and capital can be substituted to obtain the same total return. You can buy municipal bonds, expending very little labor and obtain an income. You can buy a net leased free standing Burger King and obtain an income or you can also purchase a small office building and be involved in managing the building and leasing the space or you can purchase an apartment house in a nice neighborhood and be involved as well in managing the building. Lastly, you can purchase a tenement in a poor neighborhood and commit yourself in operating it, dealing with the tenants and making the repairs. All of the above will probably produce the same amount of income. The first example requires almost no labor but a substantial amount of money. As we consider each of these examples, the amount of money required decreases but the amount of work involved increases. This is the economic reality of our times. If you do not have money you must be prepared to substitute labor as part of your investment and you will have to work hard to make up for your lack of money.

Risk–vs–Capital

If you can afford to buy municipal bonds to earn your income, you can diversify your portfolio, buy AAA rated or insured bonds, and take little or no risk in obtaining your income and preserving your assets. In seeking to obtain the same level of income with less capital, you must enlarge upon the risk which you must assume. Modern Portfolio Theory (MPT) accepts and assumes the concept that there is a direct correlation between risk and return on investment. Normally, the greater the risk the higher the return. The same is true with real estate. As you go down the ladder from a net leased free standing store leased to a rated tenant, to a luxury apartment house in a fine area of the City, to a run down tenement in a poverty area, the amount of risk becomes greater. You have a stronger probability of being successful with the first example than with the last. However, if you are willing to devote the time and effort required, the return on your investment will be much higher with the last option than with the first. It should be noted that the first example is more of a passive investment while the last example is, in reality, a very time consuming operating business. You can sit in your armchair and buy bonds but you have to be constantly involved to own and operate a distressed apartment house.

Gentrification

One of the major demographic phenomena of the past twenty years has been the gentrification of distressed areas. This trend in certain select areas, has been counter to the primary trend of such areas continuing to deteriorate. "Gentrification" happens when a higher social and economic group moves into an area containing an inferior social and economic group. The more affluent group tends to increase the housing standards and generally improves the area. One of the major causes of gentrification in the New York City area is the critical rental housing shortage, which caused the middle class to seek housing in areas, something they would not normally have considered. Another major factor leading to gentrification is the breakdown of the infrastructure of intramodal transportation from outlying areas. Commuting is becoming more and more difficult. The mass transit systems are not as efficient as they once were and the roads are in need of more repairs to compensate for deferred maintenance arising from restricted past budgets.

It is important to bear in mind that gentrification can only occur in a sophisticated urban center, where the middle class is not critically concerned about the class structure and the fear of contact with lower class elements. It is the liberal tradition that has always pervaded New York that has allowed gentrification to occur, grow and to improve the City.

There are several examples of already completed (or almost completed) gentrifications, which can be pointed to with pride in the New York area. Among these are the Upper West Side and Lower East Side of Manhattan. Both sections were in a substantial state of decline before the middle class began to move into these areas and restoring them.

The Upper West Side, the neighborhood is bounded by Riverside Drive and Riverside Park on the West and by Central Park on the East, offered large spacious apartments in what had been beautifully constructed apartment houses. The area offers many conveniences such as access to rapid transportation, numerous stores and shops, and educational and cultural institutions. The southern boundary of the Upper West Side is Lincoln Center and Fordham University, while to the north, it is Columbia University, Barnard College, The Union Theological Seminary, The Jewish Theological Seminary and Teacher's College. Broadway, which is the major commercial street in the area, has always had numerous attractive stores and shops. Columbus Avenue now offers more upscale apparel stores and fine restaurants. When gentrification first began to occur, the rents were extremely reasonable and large apartments could be obtained. Since then, gentrification has been so successful, that the rents are sky high and residential rental housing is practically unavailable. The lack of rental housing was exacerbated by a massive conversion of buildings to cooperative and condominium ownership, which eliminated much of the rental market.

Chelsea did not offer the large apartment house that the Upper West Side had, but, instead, offered available brownstones and smaller residential housing units which could be purchased for reasonable prices. The first movement in Chelsea was by those who sought to purchase their own homes, renovate them, and rent out several of the apartments so that they would be able to afford to maintain the building. Since then, apartment houses have also been purchased and renovated, and the general area has improved substantially. Eighth Avenue, which is the main thoroughfare, now boasts numerous fine shops and restaurants.

Gentrification is not limited to Manhattan, it has also occurred in parts of New Jersey, Brooklyn, and Queens. The cities of Hoboken and Hackensack in New Jersey, for instance, have gone through substantial renovation due to gentrification. These cities on the New Jersey coast facing Manhattan and now referred to as the New Jersey Gold Coast, offer the individual a chance to purchase property for very reasonable prices with easy access to Manhattan through public transportation. Jersey City, Weehawken and Edgewater are now going through the same growing pains of gentrification.

In Brooklyn, gentrification occurred first in such areas as Brooklyn Heights and Park Slope. Since then, those areas have substantially increased in value, and the cost of renting an apartment or purchasing a brownstone there has become almost prohibitive. Because of the revival of these two areas, gentrification has spread throughout the northern neighborhoods of Brooklyn. Areas such as Cobble Hill and Borum Hill, which are adjacent to Brooklyn Heights, have experienced a revival because of those individuals who sought to purchase homes for reasonable values, homes that were no longer available in Brooklyn Heights. All these sections of Brooklyn offer rapid access to Manhattan and have much esthetic appeal, which makes any and all of them attractive neighborhoods to reside.

The development of Park Slope in Brooklyn has also led to the beginning of gentrification, which is slowly occurring, in the adjacent Grand Army Plaza and in the area below Prospect Park, which is northern Flatbush. These areas once contained very fine houses and lovely smaller residential housing, which have all suffered from neglect for many years. These areas are now beginning to experience a slow and gradual revitalization, which is continuing at a start and stop pace.

The substantial increases in rent and shortage of rental housing has led to the spread of gentrification to many other areas of New York City. Among these are the Lower East Side above Houston Street and East Harlem below 116th Street in Manhattan. These areas are within close proximity to the centers of the City, and offer both the chance to purchase housing at reasonable prices and the opportunity to live in an aesthetically (but presently shabby) desirable location.

One of the major forces attracting gentrification is the fact that many distressed areas offer a double esthetic appeal in that the housing, when restored, can become beautiful, and that the area itself is physically attractive. Brooklyn Heights would be a classic example of both these factors. The brownstones in Brooklyn Heights are extremely beautiful (especially now that they have almost all been totally restored) and many offer a fine view of the Manhattan skyline and waterfront. After being fully restored, these brownstones not only become extremely attractive places to live, but offer a sense of beauty, something rarely available in other housing throughout the City.

Ethnic Gentrification

Another form of gentrification, which has been sweeping the City for many years, is the improvement of areas by specific ethnic, cultural or religious groups. Examples of this are the Poles in Greenpoint, visual artists in Soho and northern industrial Williamsburgh, gays in Chelsea and the Village, Greeks and Indians in Astoria, Hassidic Jews in Borough Park and Williamsburgh, Moslems on Atlantic Avenue, Coney Island Avenue and Yonkers, Latin American Spanish in Jackson Heights, Russians in Brighton Beach, Blacks in Bedford Stuyvesant, Albanians and Puerto Ricans in the Bronx, Cubans in Union City and the Caribbean Blacks in East Flatbush.

These ethnic and cultural groups have proceeded to occupy specific areas of the City and to mold these neighborhoods to suit their needs. They find the areas attractive as they have opportunities to live together with their own people. The stores in these neighborhoods cater to their particular needs and offer goods and services that they would not be able to obtain in other areas. Furthermore, as other members of the group seek to move into these areas, a shortage of housing is created which encourages the renovation and preservation of existing housing. This movement is directly in contrast to the older concept of the melting pot, as these individuals are seeking to preserve their identities in homogeneous neighborhoods rather in ones where they are mixed with other kinds of people. It may also be a defensive measure to avoid being harassed or abused by those different from themselves.

General Problems in Investing in Distressed Property

As stated above, purchasing property in distressed areas can be very troublesome and aggravating. Rent collection is normally slow and difficult, and the tenants are constantly complaining about lack of services and the need for repairs. Although the building may need substantial repairs, making them may not be justified by the low initial investment in the property and its actual economic value. Also, cash flow is extremely cyclical because of the high fuel expenses in winter.

It is very important to note, that although real estate in general lacks liquidity, this type of property offers extreme illiquidity. Once purchased, they it is extremely difficult to sell or refinance. Almost no bank or lending institution will give mortgages on them unless these properties are part of some government insured or subsidized program. Selling such properties also is extremely difficult as most of the purchasers are seeking to buy them with little or no cash. The normal way of selling this property is to take back a mortgage upon the property. The owner of the mortgage loan normally has a much greater financial stake in the property than the actual fee owner because the mortgage loan far exceeds the amount of equity in the property paid by the fee owner.

These areas, by being marginal, are greatly affected by the economic cycle. Their prices will fluctuate more widely than buildings in better areas. Be very careful not to buy in good times at a high price and then have to sell in bad times at a very cheap price.

7

A CASE STUDY

In this chapter we will present a classic case study of the purchase of property located within New York City at a reasonable price and with a fair chance for appreciation and growth in income. So that we will not be influenced by present events and trends, I am dating this case study back to 1981. Much research and analysis is influenced by what is occurring at the present and what the current trends are. These trends change with time just as styles change. I do not want the reader to be influenced by the present. Use the case study as a methodology for dealing with your own perceptions of the current situation in New York City. We will use the figures and demographics that were in effect at that time. At the end of this chapter, I will bring you current by informing you as to what occurred afterwards. All information regarding this study involves the late 1970s up to the year 1980. The descriptions relate to that time and not to the present.

Location

The property in question is located on Flatbush Avenue near Church Avenue in the heart of Brooklyn. The street is heavily commercial and it is difficult to find parking during the day. Although once predominantly Irish and Jewish, the neighborhood now is Black and Puerto Rican. Many Caribbean Blacks have moved into the area and have begun to take over the existing small stores on Flatbush Avenue.

Historically, Flatbush and Church Avenues have always been popular commercial streets. These have been active commercial thoroughfares for the past one hundred years. The area had been going downhill for approximately fifteen years. The stores which once had attractive displays and carried fine merchandise, now have hand painted signs and consist primarily of discounters. Macy's and Sears Roebuck still maintain large stores within the immediate area and certain chain stores are also still present.

Over the past two years, the area has begun to show signs of revitalization. Many stores are changing hands and new storefronts are being put on them. Through a program sponsored by Citibank and the City of New York, many residential buildings are being remodeled and renovated with government assistance.

Although the area is populated predominately by minorities, the streets are heavily trafficked and the people walking about look well groomed and well dressed. Everyone is in a hurry and the neighborhood appears to be bustling. Many of the stores appear to be carrying a better grade of merchandise than what has been carried in the part. Few vacancies are readily discernable on the street.

The Property

The building in question is an older commercial property, which is attached on both sides. It has a store on the ground floor and two apartments above. It is approximately twenty feet wide and occupies approximately eighty-eight feet of a one hundred foot lot. The building has three stories and an outside cellar door, which leads to the basement. The basement is totally unoccupied and there is an apartment on each side of the floors above the store. For many years the building has been owned by an absentee landlord and much deferred maintenance has accumulated on the building. Although basically sound, the heating system is not in the best of condition and the wood on the window frames is rotting.

The Tenancy

The store tenant sells health and beauty aids and appears to know his business. He has been at this location for approximately five years and has two persons working with him. One is his daughter.

The second and third floor tenants are both women with children. They are receiving assistance from social services and are quiet. Although they pay their rent late, they do pay it. They have continually complained to the landlord about repairs and their complaints are not without justification. Heating is a problem as the heat does not seem to reach the top floor. It is important to note that you are buying location and not the tenants who are residing there. In an area such as this, you will rarely find tenants who have high credit ratings considered to be reliable tenants. There is no guarantee that these tenants will continue to remain in the building. However, if the street itself is active, you can be assured that you will not have great difficulty in renting the space. It is the location that will establish the merchant, not the merchant who will establish the location.

The store should be the prime concern in purchasing this property as that is what provides the bulk of the rental from the property. It is the rent that will be obtained from the store tenant that will make the property a winner or a loser. It should be noted that the twenty footers are small stores and the least desirable. A reputable merchant would want a larger store so that he could hold more merchandise and service more customers. It is tough to make a living from such a small store and they are more suitable for the marginal or newer merchants.

The Purchase Price

After seeing several similar buildings in the neighborhood, it appears that these twenty-foot buildings sell for $40,000 to $45,000 apiece regardless of the rental obtained from the tenants on the property. Although mortgage financing is not available from a lending institution, it is customary in neighborhoods such as this for the seller to provide the financing for the purchaser.

After much negotiation, in which the seller points out that the building is heated with gas rather than oil heat and will therefore require less maintenance and that the real estate assessment if the building is only $20,000, a purchase price of $40,000 is arrived at. The purchase price is to be paid with $10,000 in cash and by the seller taking back a purchase money mortgage of $30,000. The mortgage loan is for ten years with 12% constant, consisting of interest at the rate of 10% per annum and amortization of 2%. This will require monthly payments of $300 and will have a balloon (or unpaid principal balance) at the end of its ten-year term of $19,757.75.

The Setup

The seller presents the prospective purchaser with a setup. A "setup" gives a breakdown as to the income and expenses from the building. After reviewing the setup and comparing notes with real estate brokers in the neighborhood and owners of other buildings as to the approximate maintenance costs, it appears that the income and expense statement for the building is as follows:

Rent

Store ($550 monthly)	$ 6,600
First Floor ($175 monthly)	2,100
Second Floor ($75 monthly)	900
TOTAL ANNUAL RENT:	**$ 9,600**

Expenditures

Fuel	$ 1,900
Real Estate Taxes	1,750
Insurance	950
Mortgage payments	3,600
Electricity (public hallway)	150
Repairs	500
Vacancies and Uncollected rent	500
Water and Sewer	200
TOTAL ANNUAL EXPEDITURES:	**$ 9,550**
NET CASH FLOW:	**$ 50**

The store and residential apartments appear to be rented for extremely cheap prices. No apartment should rent for $75 as it probably costs more than that to heat the unit. It is probably rented so cheaply because the present landlord provides no service and does not want the tenant bothering him. As the building has only two apartments, it is not subject to rent control or rent stabilization. As the tenants have no leases, there is little question that the landlord is allowed to raise their rentals. The store tenant's lease will expire in the very near future and should be increased.

The cost of fuel is verified by going down to Brooklyn Union Gas (now Key-span) and examining their records as to what the total fuel charges were for last year. The real estate tax charge is based on a tax rate of $8.75 per $100 of assessed valuation. As the assessed valuation of the building is $20,000 the real estate taxes will be $1,750. The insurance figure of $950 was verified with an independent broker. The mortgage payments have been negotiated by and between the parties and set at $3,600. The electricity charges were verified by checking the seller's paid bills. Repairs and vacancies were set arbitrarily by picking a figure, which is approximately 5% each of the rental income. The water and sewer charges were verified by checking with the City Collector.

Although the building at present only breaks even, it appears to offer potential for income through raising of rents. There is no guarantee that you can get increases because of the condition of the building. It should be noted that even on its present basis, there is something to be said for the building. Even at break even there is amortization of the mortgage loan so that even if there is not money in our pocket, a small amount is also being applied each month to reduce our lia-bilities. Needless to say this is a small sum of money, not really worth all the bother and aggravation, but it is a start. No taxable income is generated by this amortization because if we allocate $5,000 to the land and $35,000 to the build-ing, there will be sufficient depreciation to offset the annual pay down of princi-pal from the operations of the building, which is not costing us anything out of pocket.

One year later

We now look back on the building one year after it has been purchased and we are able to produce the following income and expense statement:

Rent

Store ($650 monthly)	$ 7,800
First Floor ($200 monthly)	2,400
Second Floor ($150 monthly)	1,800
TOTAL ANNUAL RENT:	**$ 12,000**

Expenditures

Fuel	$ 2,400
Real estate Taxes	1,750
Insurance	1,100
Mortgage payments	3,600
Electricity	225
Repairs	750
Vacancies and Uncollected rents	-0-
Water and Sewer	200

TOTAL ANNUAL EXPENDITURES: **$ 10,025**

NET CASH FLOW: **$ 1,975**

It would appear that the building has prospered. The new owner of the buildings has been able to increase the rentals of the tenants to bring them more up to date. It should be noted that a five-year lease was signed with the store tenant providing for rentals for the five years of the lease as follows: $650 monthly for the first two years, $700 for the next two years and $750 for the last year of the lease term. The residential tenants have signed one-year leases and the landlord intends to increase their rentals at the expiration of their leases.

Fuel costs have increased, which increase is beyond the landlord's control as it has been caused by a general increase in the price of natural gas. Insurance premium costs have also increased, but considering the neighborhood, the landlord is happy that he has insurance. Although the landlord was very fortunate in that the tenants did not vacate and stiff him for a few months rent, when he asked for increased rents, his repair bill did exceed his estimate.

It appears that this building was a good choice for this investor, and that it will continue to increase in cash flow and value with the passing of time.

A look back from the future

We can now look back to this investment fifteen years later and see what actually occurred. A rejuvenation began at the Flatbush Avenue shopping district and prices bloomed. The new landlord, being under-capitalized, did not have enough money to make the necessary renovations in the building to attract a quality tenant. In addition, if the existing store tenant vacated the premises, the new landlord did not have sufficient funds to wait with a vacant store for a good solid new tenant. Furthermore, the investor was a professional and found that he was taking up too much time in running the building and that it was eating into his practice. He could not afford the time involved. The investor sold the building for $85,000 of which $25,000 was paid in cash and the balance of $60,000 with a 12% interest ten year self amortizing purchase money mortgage loan.

The new purchaser only kept the building for two years and then sold it for $150,000 to a storekeeper who bought the building for his own use. This is called a "user." The user fully remodeled the building and still occupies it to this very day.

Prices and rents skyrocketed in the area but then fell with the decline in real estate values in the late 1980s. Even today, an average store such as this one rents for $2,500 to $3,500 monthly, and the buildings sell from $250,000 to $300,000. It is unfortunate that the investor did not just sit and wait.

Notes to Financial Projections

Projections are fine but do not imagine that they are as accurate as they appear. It is nice to talk of returns of 18.07% but they should be used only as a guideline and nothing else. The decimal points are there to deceive you into thinking it is an exact calculation, when, in reality, there is no such thing. One small repair or the loss of one rental can completely knock these figures out of whack. Finance men going into real estate often rely too heavily upon projections, and by doing so have lost substantial sums of money. At best, projections can give you a very rough idea, or point in the direction in which the investment should be heading if everything is on schedule and proceeds more or less as you anticipated.

These figures do not include any capital improvements, which the landlord may choose to make. It might be wise to invest money in the beginning to paint the window trim and cornice, or to overhaul the heating plant. Storm windows might be a sound investment and a new roof could be critical. The investor can either consider these capital improvements as an expense, and just chalk them up to the initial expenses in renovating the building, or else the investor can add this to the cost of purchasing the building and consider this to be part of his purchase price. No one expects to purchase a building in perfect condition. Money must be spent to bring the property up to par.

General Observation

In general, if you buy in the right location, time will bail you out. Rents will increase and make the building profitable. In the area we just examined, the only competition for buildings is from users who purchase buildings for their own use. In this neighborhood, many storekeepers are beginning to make substantial improvements in their stores and want to own the buildings in which they are making improvements rather than spend money fixing up someone else's property. They also want the security of not having to worry about moving their businesses when leases expire. A user can afford to pay more for a building than an investor because the building has much greater value for someone who will be operating his own business in the location. Also, users tend to upgrade the areas in which they are located as they have a direct financial investment in the community.

This is also true with residential property. When a neighborhood undergoes revitalization, many of the small brownstones, which had six to ten tenants, are converted into two and three family homes, with the owner occupying one of the apartments. This is always a sure sign that a residential neighborhood is improving.

8

THE PROCEDURE FOR PURCHASING PROPERTY

Purchasing property is slightly more complex, and involves more initiative and work, than other investments. It is relatively simple to purchase shares of stock, for instance. All you have to do is call up your broker and complete the transaction on the telephone. Purchasing real property, on the other hand, requires a great deal of effort on the part of the purchaser. In this Chapter we will examine the entire process of purchasing property, from the search for available property through the completion of the purchase and obtaining title.

The search for property

Before even beginning to look for a specific property to purchase, the investor should have a fairly good idea as to the type of property he is seeking to purchase. A preliminary strategy should be developed by the investor so that he will not be looking at random but will have a specific idea as to what he is searching for. In narrowing down the range of perspective investments, the potential purchaser may seek to limit his range to a specific geographic area, or to a type of real estate. For example, the investor may be seeking to purchase a walk up apartment house with less than twenty apartments on the east side of Manhattan between Houston Street and 14th Street, and from Avenue A to Third Avenue. Another example might be the investor who is seeking to purchase a net leased gas station in the greater New York area. In any event, the investor must first try and locate suitable properties which are available for sale.

Advertisements

One of the best ways to look for property is to purchase the Sunday edition of The New York Times and to study the real estate classified section. This contains listings of various properties available for sale throughout the greater metropolitan area. The listings are divided by geographic area and type of property. For example, there is a special section dealing with apartment houses which is further subdivided by borough. One need only look for Apartment Houses—Queens to discover whether any apartment houses are available in Queens County. Even if there is nothing available of interest to you, the buildings which are available are frequently listed by brokers, and you can call these real estate brokers to see if they have anything else available which they had not advertised. This is a relatively easy way of doing things as one can stay comfortably at home reading through the classified sections. The Sunday Times can be purchased on Saturday night if you are particularly eager and want to be ready to start inquiring on Sunday.

The difficult part is that all advertisements are geared to sell and the seller or broker who placed the advertisement may not be truly stating the quality of the building, or may be leaving certain matters unsaid. If the advertisement looks interesting, the prospective purchaser should call the number indicated or write to the address listed to obtain more details. During the initial conversation or letter, the prospective purchaser should attempt to ascertain the exact address of the property, the purchase price, the available terms being sought, how much the building is earning and a detailed income and expense statement. Normally, after the initial contact with the seller or broker, the purchaser will be sent a listing describing all the relevant details. Please note that this listing may or may not be accurate and must be verified by the purchaser. The purchaser must go out and physically inspect the property to ascertain exactly what condition the property is in and the quality of the immediate neighborhood. In further examination and in verification of the information given by the seller or broker, the purchaser may request to inspect the fuel bills, real estate tax bills and tenant leases relating to the building.

Signs

Another way of finding property available for sale is to walk through a neighborhood and notice signs placed upon buildings indicating that the property is for sale. Generally, this is found with smaller buildings. You will not find a For Sale sign upon a large house or office building. Many of these signs are placed by real estate brokers acting on behalf of the seller. The prospective purchaser should write down the phone number and the name listed on the sign and should then call the telephone number to obtain further information. Although this is somewhat more time-consuming than reading the classified section of the newspaper, it does allow the investor to see the exact building before commencing any further negotiations or inquiries. If the neighborhood or building are not desirable, or not reflected in the price being asked, then the purchaser will move on and look for another available building, and may not even bother calling the number listed on the sign.

Real Estate Brokers

Real estate brokers can be very helpful in locating property to purchase. They tend to specialize either by type of property or by neighborhood, and they usually know what is available for sale within their specialty. It is important for a real estate broker to know this if he hopes to earn commissions by selling properties. Brokers, in general, tend to be very knowledgeable about the properties they have for sale and are fully familiar with the current market prices for them.

It is important to remember that a real estate broker only gets paid if he makes a sale and will always do his best to sell a property. It must always be kept in mind that the broker has a strong bias in favor of making the sale. You should therefore not always believe everything a broker tells you. As in any other industry, there are good brokers and bad ones, honest brokers and dishonest ones. It is critically important for you to find a real estate broker not only whom you regard as knowledgeable but whom you can trust.

A competent broker can save you much time and effort because he can rapidly sift and find properties available for sale at realistic prices and not just for show. Many sellers place their properties on the market with no actual intention of making a sale. They do this to obtain a price substantially above the market only then will they consider selling; otherwise, they deal with prospective purchasers only to find out how much they are prepared to pay. In essence, are using such persons only to conduct their own market surveys. This is an exercise in futility for the purchaser, and a broker can eliminate such "sellers" for you. Furthermore, a broker may be able to assist in obtaining financing, and even in locating prospective tenants for a building with any vacancies.

The Area

Once you have narrowed down your choices extreme care should be paid to the area in which the building is located. Many substantial investors believe that this is more important than the actual condition of the building. Even if the neighborhood appears homogeneous, there tend to be differences from block to block. The only way of telling whether the area meets your criteria is to take a walking tour. Driving through the area is not sufficient. Get out and walk the streets. Stop in at a restaurant or coffee shop and order something to eat while speaking to people in the shop, if they are not too busy. You should also consider stopping and talking to tenants in front of the building, or to shop keepers in the area. Through casual conversations you can often obtain critical input as to what is presently going on in the neighborhood.

It is not enough to visit an area just once before making a purchase, as you may pick a day that is not typical for some reason. Several visits should be made, and conversations should be initiated with a number of people to determine what is happening in the neighborhood and whether it is prospering. Many neighborhoods might appear to be solid but in reality are decaying. Likewise, many areas which appear to be devastated, may have actually bottomed out and are beginning to revitalize themselves.

The Building

After you are satisfied with the area, you should then direct your attention to a physical examination of the building. It is very important that you determine whether the building is in proper physical condition or money must be spent to rehabilitate it. It is a plus if the building has some aesthetic appeal, but such appeal may serve to hide certain major defects within.

Many buildings are uneconomical because of their physical layout. The room size of the apartments may be too large and you may not be able to obtain a rental commensurate with their size. Likewise, the stores located in the building may be set up in such a manner that prevents you from attracting a tenant who will pay the appropriate rent. A substantial store tenant, for instance, requires a relatively deep store so that he can have a place to keep his merchandise.

The nature of the use of the building is also critically important. If there is no demand for the way in which the building is being used by its present occupants, you must give consideration to making substantial alterations which will better serve the community. If the building is situated in an area where factory buildings are dying out and giving way to residential buildings, then you will have to be prepared to expend a large sum of money to convert a factory to residential use. However, if the building is already serving a use which is in demand in that community, then the building will serve a suitable purpose, and in all probability generate a commensurate return.

Purchase Terms

After you have decided that the building and neighborhood are suitable for investment, careful scrutiny should be given to the proposed offering price and terms for purchasing the building. The price being asked should show some corresponding relationship with the income being generated by the building and the cash being required for purchasing the building. Most investment buildings being sold are not sold for all cash, but for a proportion in cash with the seller taking back the balance in the form of a purchase money mortgage loan.

It is important that the prospective purchaser analyze the relationship of cash flow to the amount of cash being required in the purchase price. This is commonly called the "cash on cash return." If an investor is able to earn a $1,000 return on an investment of $10,000, then he realizes a 10% cash flow on his initial cash investment, or a 10% cash on cash return. Normally speaking, the smaller the cash portion of the purchase price, the greater the cash on cash return. This is called leverage and it works both ways. If there is any small decline in the operating income of the building, the cash flow will not be sufficient to provide any return at all, and in order to satisfy the mortgage loan requirements, the purchaser will have to put in additional money of his own. If there is more cash and less mortgage, then the leverage will be less, the mortgage payments will be less and there is a greater probability that the building will be able to withstand a downturn in operating income and still survive without the need for additional funds. Normally speaking, offering more cash will result in a lower purchase price because the seller will feel more secure knowing that he has a smaller purchase money mortgage loan and that the purchaser has more equity in the building.

A property may be a great investment but if you pay too much, it no longer is that good an investment. The investor should be careful to purchase property at a reasonable price. If he is too stingy and looks only for bargains, then he will find himself unable to purchase any property at all, or only properties which have serious problems. Normally, there is a fluid market for the purchase and sale of property, and a parcel priced at an extremely cheap level will find numerous individuals with a keen interest in purchasing it. It is normally not good to look for bargains in purchasing real property as they are rarely available. The first-time purchaser should seek to buy a property for a fair and reasonable price rather than to seek an absolute bargain. If the investor purchases well, and the building and area continue along the trends he has projected, then he will realize a handsome return on his investment as time passes.

Making an Offer

After the purchaser has determined what price and terms he is prepared to pay for the property, he should then make an offer of purchase to the seller. If a real estate broker is involved then the offer should be made through the broker. It is at this time that a good real estate broker can be very helpful as he is in a position to act as a middle man, going back and forth between the buyer and seller in trying to narrow any difference of price and terms. The real estate broker may tell the seller that he is seeking too high a price and the purchaser that his bids are too low.

The negotiations between the purchaser and seller may not only involve price but also the amount of cash required, and the terms and conditions of any purchase money mortgage. Rather than reduce the price, the seller may reduce the amount of the cash and increase the amount of the mortgage he is willing to give. Also, the seller can reduce the rate of interest being charged on the mortgage, or may stretch out the amortization of the mortgage rather than reduce the price. For example, if the seller has been offering his property for $200,000 with $40,000 in cash and the balance in the form of a $160,000 purchase money mortgage bearing interest at the rate of 10% per annum and self-amortizing over ten years, then rather than reduce the price, the seller may offer the building for the same $200,000 but with $20,000 cash and a $180,000 purchase money mortgage bearing interest at the rate of 8% per annum and self-amortizing over fifteen years. This has the effect of increasing the cash flow being generated by the property as it has reduced the cost of servicing the mortgage. This increased cash flow may justify the price being asked by the seller. The reverse is also true, a seller may reduce the purchase price if he receives better and higher purchase money terms.

The Binder

Many brokers request that a purchaser make a small deposit and sign a binder agreeing to purchase the property for a specified price but with very general terms. The normal purpose of such binders is to obtain a signed good faith deposit and agreement from the purchaser. These binders are very dangerous and should be avoided whenever possible. Either a binder is a meaningless document or it is actually a contract of sale, as many courts have so held. If it is a meaningless document, then there is no purpose served in signing such a document and in giving a deposit. If, on the other hand, a binder is so detailed that a Court may deem it to be a contract of sale, it becomes a highly dangerous paper to sign. It is foolish to tie up a substantial piece of property with a down payment of only $500 or a $1,000 as usually provided for in binders. Before signing a binder an attorney should be consulted. It at all possible, the purchaser ought to refuse to sign the binder, and should inform the seller or broker that he wishes to proceed immediately to sign a contract of sale and to make a more substantial down payment.

Binders are basically a gimmick dreamed up by real estate brokers so that they may know how many people are seriously interested in a piece of property. It is not uncommon for a broker to hold two, three or even five binders on the same property. If the first contract of sale is not finalized or falls through, then the broker will proceed to the next individual who gave a binder.

The Contract

The contract is the most important document to be entered into in connection with purchasing property. It sets forth all the terms and conditions of the purchase the price of the property with the terms of any purchase money financing or other existing financing are specified. Likewise, the contract sets forth the obligations of the seller to deliver good and remarketable title to the property. Any of the terms of the contract of sale are negotiable, and it is important to obtain the services of a knowledgeable real estate attorney when negotiating the contract. At the signing of the contract, the purchaser normally makes a down payment on the purchase price. This down payment is usually equivalent to 10% of the total price. For example, if a purchaser is purchasing a building for $250,000, he will normally pay $25,000 at that time to the seller. Many attorneys insist, quite correctly, that the payment made on contract be held in escrow by the attorney for the seller until the closing of title. In the event that the purchaser is unable to obtain good title to the property, his deposit on contract will then be immediately returned by the attorney.

Obtaining a Mortgage

Many contracts are conditional upon the purchaser being able to obtain a mortgage on the property. This is normally the case when a building is being purchased for the residential use of the purchaser. The buyer of a cooperative apartment for $200,000, for instance, may not have the full $200,000 for making the purchase. He might only have $60,000 but may also have a good job and will be able to make the necessary payments on a mortgage. If this fact is known to both the buyer and the seller, and the seller understands that the purchaser is not able to purchase the property unless he can obtain the difference between the amount of cash he has available and the purchase price from a lending institution, the contract will be made conditional upon the purchaser obtaining the required financing from a lending institution within a specified period of time. Should the purchaser be unable to obtain the financing, then the contract will be deemed null and void, and his payment on contract will be returned to him. In the event that the purchaser does obtain the financing, then the contract will be in full force and effect, and the purchaser will be required to proceed and purchase the property from the seller.

Title Insurance

It is customary in New York for the purchaser's attorney to order a title insurance report from a title company prior to the closing and to submit this report to the seller's attorney prior to the closing. Rather than relying upon the purchaser's attorney to examine all the documents and records to ascertain whether or not the seller has good and marketable title, it is common in New York for the purchaser to instruct his attorney to order a title report from a title company and to obtain title insurance at the closing. The title reports sets forth all and any exceptions to title, which the seller may have. For example, the title company will make a search and report all existing mortgages upon the property which is being purchased free of all mortgages, then the seller will have to remove these mortgages prior to closing. Likewise, there may also be a judgment entered and docketed against the seller which affects his property, and this judgment will have to be satisfied prior to the closing.

At the closing, a representative of the title insurance company will be present, and he will insure the results of his report at that time. The purpose of this insurance is to make certain that the purchaser is obtaining exactly what he expected to purchase pursuant to the terms of the contract of sale. Should it later be discovered that one of the deeds in the chain of title was forged, then the title company will have to compensate the purchaser in the event that the property is taken away from him. Also, should the title company insure that certain real estate taxes were paid, if they were not, the title company, and not the purchaser, will have the obligation to pay these real estate taxes. Title insurance remains in effect as long as the purchaser continues to own the property. Upon sale of the property, the title insurance expires and the new purchaser must obtain his own title insurance. The price of title insurance is fairly reasonable and the prospective purchaser should regard it as a necessity.

The Closing

The final act of purchasing the property comes at the closing when the seller transfers the deed to the purchaser. The deed is a relatively simple piece of paper, which describes the property and states that the seller is transferring this property to the purchaser.

Numerous other papers and documents will be involved at the closing. If there are any purchase money mortgages, the purchaser will sign the mortgage and mortgage note at that time as well as all other papers and documents relating to it. If there are tenants in the property, the seller will request that the purchaser acknowledge receipt of each tenant's security deposit and agree to identify the seller with respect to same. Also, a letter will be sent to all tenants notifying them as to the change of ownership. The representative of the title company will also be present, and he will insure and certify that title in the property has been transferred to the purchaser. He will also take all the relevant documents which are to be recorded, and will collect all these and any taxes required with respect to the transfer of the property.

Adjustments

At the closing, all adjustments will be made with respect to the operation of the property. The seller of the property may be paying real estate taxes at the rate of $1,500 every three months. If the real estate taxes are due on January 1st and they are for a three month period and the closing takes place on February 1st then the seller is entitled to receive the return of $1,000 of the $1,500 which he paid for real estate taxes, as he will have only owned the property for one month of the three-month period for which real estate taxes have been paid. Likewise, adjustments are made with respect to fuel, water and sewer charges, rents received from tenants, and insurance premiums affecting the property. These costs of operating the property are normally adjusted as of the date of closing and are broken down to a *per diem* (daily) rate. It should be also noted that if the property is being sold subject to an existing mortgage, then the accrued interest expense upon this mortgage is also adjusted. Adjustments are also made with respect to the payment made by the purchaser at the signing of the contract and are deducted from the total purchase price.

When all the figures are taken into account, a net balance is normally derived. This is usually in favor of the seller and the purchaser is required to make this final net payment in cash, or by certified or bank check. The reason for this is so the seller will not have to be concerned about the purchaser's check being dishonored. Normally, the purchaser and seller want little to do with each other after the transaction is completed. The seller only wants to know that he has sold the building, and the purchaser that he has purchased the building. The certified check insures that all final monies being paid are available and that there will be no problems.

Closing Costs

Closing costs in New York include title insurance, recording the deed and mortgage, the mortgage and real property transfer taxes, and any relevant adjustments. These can add up to be a substantial amount, and in New York it is relatively expensive to purchase or sell property. The seller must pay a real property transfer tax as well as a New York State transfer tax. The purchaser has to pay a mortgage tax upon all mortgages obtained at closing.

These costs should be paid only when you intend to hold the property for a long time and can amortize them over the life of the property; otherwise, they will seem to be extremely high. Such costs thus tend to discourage real estate as a short-term investment. The purchase and sale of real property is expensive and the costs of buying or selling greatly detract from any profit which may be made in the short term.

It is therefore critical for you to be fully aware that real estate, in general, is not a way of turning a quick dollar, and that any investor in real estate should be patient, and be willing to plan for the long term.

9

COOPERATIVES AND CONDOMINIUMS

With the rising prosperity Americans have experienced over the past forty years, more and more people are seeking to own their homes. Those who cannot afford a small home on a piece of property must content themselves to own an attached one family house, perhaps with a small garden in the back. With the increasing cost of land near urban centers, even small attached homes have become prohibitively expensive for many. To overcome this, and still be the owners of their own homes, more people are now seeking to purchase the apartments in which they live. Depending on the form of ownership, such purchases of individual units are called co-operatives or condominiums.

The Nature of a Co-operative

A Co-operative is an apartment house in which all the tenants own shares of stock in the corporation, which owns the building. With their shares, they also receive a proprietary lease. This gives them the right to occupy their apartments. In reality, the purchaser of a co-operative apartment does not own his apartment; rather he owns shares of stock in the co-operative corporation which owns the building in which his apartment is located. These shares will be proportionate to the reasonable value of his apartment in comparison with the other apartments in the building. It is the lease to his apartment, which is normally assigned simultaneously with the transfer of the shares of stock, that gives him the right to occupy his apartment. There may be an existing mortgage upon the entire building and the tenant may also obtain additional financing when be buys his particular apartment. The mortgage on the building is very similar to any other mortgage, such as we have already discussed. The loan for the purchase of the tenant's apartment is called a co-op loan and it is secured by an assignment of the tenant's shares of stock in the co-operative corporation as well as the assignment of his proprietary lease to the apartment. Should the tenant fail to pay the co-op loan, the lending institution may take his shares of stock and his lease, and obtain possession of his apartment. The default will not trigger any problems for the apartment house itself, as it is the tenant who has borrowed money from the lending institution to purchase his apartment. In a co-op everything is highly centralized and almost all decisions lie with the Board of Directors of the corporation. Each tenant is only a shareholder in the corporation, which owns the building, and he is entitled to vote only the number of shares he owns. A decision as to whether or not to refinance, or to increase the existing mortgage upon the building, will be a decision of all the shareholders. The tenant will be entitled to vote only his shares of stock. He may be outvoted, or he may find that other shareholders have voted like him. Individual tenants, in reality, have very little control over whether the co-op should add additional mortgage financing to its building. This additional financing will increase the maintenance charges of all the tenants as the monthly interest and amortization payments will be allocated among the shareholders, and be charged to each tenant in proportion to the number of shares he owns. In New York City, the financing charges paid upon the underlying mortgage play an important part in determining the total maintenance charges for the building. On average, mortgage costs may equal up to 40% of the total maintenance charges of the building. Since each tenant has little control over the mortgage upon the building, each loses substantial control over the monitoring of his individual maintenance charges. Also, you cannot sell or rent your apartment without approval of the Co-op's Board of Directors.

The Nature of the Condominium

Condominiums are similar in intent to co-ops, except that they offer an individual tenant more freedom of decision. Each condominium owner has actual title to his apartment. He is not a shareholder in a corporation which owns the building. Rather he owns his apartment outright. In conjunction with the other apartment owners, the tenant becomes part of the condominium association that operates and manages the building as do all the others. He will always have a say in the operation of the building which will be in proportion to the value of his apartment relative to all the others in the building. There can be no underlying mortgages on a building set up for condominium ownership, as each apartment is really a separate "building" in itself. Every tenant has both the responsibility and right to obtain for his apartment through whatever financing he desires. Some tenants will elect to take none at all and will buy their apartments outright, without a mortgage, while others will seek to obtain the highest mortgage available. Needless to say, the amount of financing obtained will affect the cost of maintaining the apartment. A tenant who opts for considerable financing will have higher maintenance charges than one who requires little or no financing. This is an election to be made by each individual tenant and is not dependent upon the consensus of opinion of the other unit owners. The loan is obtained by the tenant on his condominium unit and it is the equivalent of a mortgage loan. By contrast, the loan obtained by a tenant on his co-operative apartment is the equivalent of a personal loan secured by personal assets, namely, his lease and shares of stock. The sale of a condominium unit is similar to the sale of a one-family house, and involves a full closing. Usually, no consent is required to rent or sell your apartment, and the purchaser or tenant does not have to be approved.

The Benefits of Ownership

Ownership of a co-operative apartment or a condominium unit offers substantial benefits. In a co-op, all real estate taxes and mortgage interest payments, paid by the co-operative corporation may be passed through to its shareholders and become deductible from their income taxes. Furthermore, a substantial portion of the maintenance charges paid by co-op owners consist of real estate taxes on the building and the mortgage interest payments on the underlying mortgage on the building. These payments are directly deductible by the tenant.

Condominium ownership provides for even more direct tax benefits as each owner is able to deduct the real estate taxes paid directly on his individual unit as well as any mortgage interest payments. The net effect of such deductions reduces the effective maintenance charge for the apartment. In reality, part of the maintenance costs are paid by the government which is allowing the tenant a tax deduction for real estate taxes and mortgage interest payments. If a rental apartment carries the same rent as the maintenance charges paid on a co-op, the tenant in the co-op will find that after taxes he is paying less in maintenance charges than what the rent would have been.

Another substantial advantage of ownership is that the tenant derives benefits from any repairs or improvements he makes in his apartment. In an ordinary rental apartment, if the tenant breaks down walls or makes substantial changes in the apartment, he may be required to expend money when he vacates the premises to restore the apartment to its original condition. This will apply even if the improvement had the effect of making the apartment appear more attractive. In a co-op or condominium, any improvements made by the tenant will be reflected in a better selling price of the apartment. If the tenant made substantial improvements in his apartment that increase its aesthetic appeal, he benefits.

Conversions in New York City

The past twenty-five years have seen massive conversions of apartment houses in New York City to co-operative or condominium ownership. In most of the country, condominium ownership is the more prevalent form. In New York City co-operative ownership has become by far the more popular form of ownership. Although most of the conversions occurred in Manhattan, there have been numerous successful conversions in Brooklyn, Queens and in certain portions of the Bronx as well as in the suburbs.

The shortage of affordable one-family homes for young couples, particularly within reasonable commuting distance to work in the urban center, has greatly added to the attraction of owning an apartment in Manhattan. Rather than purchase an apartment in some outlying suburb with a difficult to commute, many people prefer to live closer in their own apartments. Landlords also benefited by converting their buildings, as they saw that selling co-operative apartments, or condominium units, to individual tenants brought a much higher price for the building, than were they to have if they sold the entire building to a single buyer. Indeed, owners believed that they could sell retail for a higher price than selling wholesale. Unfortunately they discovered that selling retail is difficult, and many had great difficulty in selling all of their apartments. They frequently sold some but not enough to bail them out. The majority of the apartments went unsold, and they were left holding them while dealing with a co-op board which represented a minority ownership of the building but still was able to effectuate control over the entire building and over the landlord's unsold apartments. What many sponsors of conversions thought would be a bonanza turned out to be a major headache and a continuing problem.

In addition, the cost of maintaining an apartment house has increased greatly over the years while rentals have not been permitted to increase at the same rate. The Rent Control Law and Rent Stabilization regulations that exist in New York City put a ceiling on increases a landlord may obtain for his apartments. Many rents received by landlords do not fully compensate them for their expenses. Rather than fight the system, many a landlord therefore chose to sell his buildings to his tenants and thereby obtain a higher price. Once a building is owned by the tenants, they can set the maintenance at any level they consider necessary. Many tenants do not mind paying higher maintenance charges when they understand that this is the cost of maintaining their property and protecting their ownership interest.

Even after conversion, providing it is a non-eviction plan (which most are), the existing rent controlled or rent stabilized tenants who do not choose to buy their apartments are still protected by the law from increases above their rent guidelines. All future tenants who move into the building after the conversion, even if they are renting and did not buy their apartments can be charged any rent which the renter of the apartment can obtain. This applies to apartments that are sub-leased by individuals who purchased their apartments, and also by the sponsor of the plan who is renting unsold units.

It is only now, in the present housing boom, that sponsors are able to sell apartments at a substantial profit. For many years sponsors just sat on their apartments and rented them to tenants when they could not find purchasers to pay reasonable prices.

What makes an apartment valuable?

Many criteria are used to which determine the value of an individual apartment. The most important is the desirability and location of the building itself. If the building is in a prime residential area it will have substantially more value than one not in as good a neighborhood. In addition, some buildings have more status and prestige. Normally, an apartment in a building which has an elite group of tenants will have greater value than one in a building with ordinary working tenants. For this reason, many tenant groups are very careful when interviewing new applicants who wish to purchase an apartment. Most co-op Boards require a prospective purchaser to submit financial statements and letters of recommendation.

As further protection for the building, many tenant groups insist that a purchaser of an apartment in their building, purchase the apartment with no more than 50% financing, some even require purchasers to pay all cash without any outside financing. They want to make sure that the purchaser is financially able to maintain his apartment. In the event that there is any dispute about whether or not to increase maintenance charges, or whether to have an additional doorman, they want to know that no tenant will vote against doing so on the basis of lack of an inability to pay the increased cost. Many buildings are also very concerned about safety, and doormen are maintained at the premises more for safety than for convenience. Employing a doorman does not involve one salary but actually four as you need three doormen for each twenty-four hour shift, and since each doorman receives two days off a week with vacation and sick days an additional doorman is also needed. Doormen, as you can see, are a considerable expense.

Needless to say, the size and location of the apartment in the building will also have a great effect upon determining its value. The larger the apartment, the more it is worth. This increase in value is more likely to be geometric than arithmetic. A three-bedroom apartment is worth substantially more than three one-bedroom apartments. This is because most buildings have mainly small apartments and large apartments are relatively rare. The higher the floor an apartment is on, the more valuable it becomes, as it will usually have a better view than one on a lower floor. Should the apartment have a park view, or of a body of water, this will also add to its value.

It should be noted that within any given building, generally, the more valuable the apartment, the higher the maintenance charges. This is because shares of stock in co-operative apartment houses are allocated to each apartment on the basis of its reasonable value in relationship with other apartments in the building. From time to time abnormalities will develop and there will be an apartment which is more valuable than another but will have fewer shares and therefore a lower value. The Attorney General (New York State Department of Law) and the Internal Revenue Service require that in obtaining a co-operative status, the number of shares allocated to each apartment should bear a reasonable relationship.

Some apartment houses that seem similar, have lower maintenance charges than others. There are a variety of reasons for this. An older apartment house may have a substantially reduced underlying mortgage and this reduces the average maintenance charges for each apartment. Older buildings may also have lower real estate tax assessment charges, which also reduce maintenance. A newer building, on the other hand, may have lower repair costs, which can reduce its maintenance charges. It is important for a potential purchaser of a co-op or condominium to review the financial statements of the building in order to determine the component expenses comprising the maintenance charges. The minutes of the Board of Directors for the past two years should also be reviewed for any major improvements that may be on the horizon. It could well be that the building has low maintenance charges because it has an existing mortgage loan bearing a very low rate of interest. But this loan may mature in a few years and be replaced with a loan bearing current market rates, which could be substantially higher.

In general, living in a co-operative or condominium offers the tenant the benefits of living with a better and less transient class of tenant. The purchasers of apartments tend to have more pride of ownership and seek to maintain their building in better condition. The very fact that each tenant has purchased his apartment means that such tenants may, in general, be of a higher economic class. Owners of co-ops or condos tend to spend more money on improving their apartments. The very fact that each tenant must purchase his apartment before moving in and must sell his apartment before moving out, provides for greater stability of tenancy as well as less transience.

It is not uncommon to find disputes have developed in many buildings between various segments of the tenant population. Some tenants may want the maintenance charges of the building stringently controlled, while others will want to increase the maintenance charges to retain a high standard of quality within the building. There may be a dispute about whether to obtain a mortgage in order to make improvements in the building. It is always best to avoid a building that has a history of tenant disputes.

How a Building is Converted to Co-operative Ownership

The decision to convert a building to co-operative ownership is usually made by the landlord. In New York City, however, it is not uncommon for the tenants as a group to approach the landlord and ask him to sell them the building pursuant to a tenant sponsored co-op plan. Whoever offers the building as a co-op is called the "sponsor" whose first duty is to prepare a preliminary offering plan setting forth all terms and conditions of the conversion. This offering plan will contain the rights and duties of purchasers, of existing tenants in the building, of the then landlord, and of the sponsor. It will contain detailed financial statements of the building's present operating expenses and projected operating expenses. It will detail all mortgages upon the property and the rentals being received from the existing tenants. It will also contain the contract between the owner of the property and the newly formed co-operative corporation, a copy of the proprietary lease, the by-laws of the co-operative corporation, and the subscription agreement which is to be signed by all prospective purchasers. The preliminary offering plan should contain every bit of information needed to be known by each tenant and any other prospective purchasers before they decide whether to purchase an apartment. The offering plan will also contain a report from an architect and engineer detailing the physical condition of the building.

There are two primary types of offering plans: "eviction" and "non-eviction." Under an eviction plan, the sponsor will be able to evict from the building all rent controlled or rent stabilized tenants who do not purchase their apartments, except for rent controlled tenants who are disabled or over sixty-two years of age. With a non-eviction plan, all tenants are allowed to remain in possession of their apartments even if they do not purchase them. Such apartments will either be held by the sponsor, or purchased at reduced prices by individuals who can then collect rent from the existing tenants while owning the apartments subject to the occupancy of the existing tenant. These are called an "occupied apartments." An eviction plan requires the sponsor to obtain a higher percentage of tenants to be in favor of it than one with a non-eviction plan. But with the non-eviction plan, the sponsor need only obtain a minimum of 15% of the tenants to purchase apartments. In the case of an eviction plan, the sponsor must obtain 51% of the tenants purchasing their apartments.

If the sponsor does not obtain the requisite number of tenants to purchase apartments, the plan will fail. Historically, most sponsors elected to offer non-eviction plans as they had more confidence in selling 15% of the apartments rather than 51%.

Normally, to induce tenants to purchase their apartments, the sponsor will offer the tenants apartments at prices substantially below market. This is to induce the tenants to purchase apartments even through the sponsor knows that many of them will be reselling their apartments to outsiders, and thereby making a profit at fair market value. It is not uncommon for existing tenants to be allowed to purchase their apartments for 1/3 to 1/2 of the prevailing market price for similar apartments. The purchase price for these apartments is known as the "insider" price.

Any prospective purchaser would be well advised to carefully review the preliminary offering plan. Particular attention should be given to the price being asked and what the maintenance charge will be if the offering plan becomes effective. Detailed care should be given to reviewing the need for repairs in the building. Many of these buildings have substantial deferred maintenance and much money will be needed to restore the building to proper condition. As an additional incentive to prospective apartment purchasers, the sponsor may also offer to finance part of the purchase price. Such financing is normally at below market rates and is a great inducement to those tenants who may not be able to obtain financing.

This preliminary offering plan along with the accountant's, architect's and real estate expert's reports must be submitted to the New York State Department of Law (i.e. the Attorney General) for review. Only after it has been examined and the Attorney General has fully reviewed the offering plan and corrections are made by the sponsor will the Attorney General allow the offering plan to be accepted for filing.

After filing copies are sent to all the tenants in the building and the sponsor is then allowed to solicit purchasers for apartments in the building. When the sponsor has sold a specified number, he will be allowed to declare the offering plan effective, and to convey title of the apartment house to the co-operative corporation. Any apartments not sold will be deemed unsold shares and will become the responsibility of the sponsor. He will have to pay the maintenance charges on them and to arrange for their sale at a later date. In other words, the sponsor takes the risk of possibly being stuck with any unsold apartments.

Other Kinds of Co-ops

Beside apartment houses, there are many other types of buildings being converted to condominium or co-operative ownership. Office buildings, for instance, have been converted to condominium ownership in which each business enterprise owns its own space. This gives greater assurance to the business tenant that he can remain in possession and need not worry about what will happen when the lease expires. Commercial co-ops and condos, as opposed to residential ones, are not all that advantageous. A commercial business can deduct its rent in full as a business expense and does not need co-operative ownership to be able to deduct a portion of its maintenance expenses. In residential buildings, an owner of a co-operative apartment gets to deduct part of his maintenance for tax purposes while a rental tenant is not allowed to deduct anything.

Because of the extreme housing shortage in New York City, many buildings which were not apartment houses have been converted first into residential housing, and then into co-ops. Many office buildings in Manhattan's financial district have been converted into apartment houses and sold as co-ops. In the area above the financial district, and going up to 34th Street, there are numerous loft buildings which no longer serve any viable commercial function. New York City was once a center for garment manufacturing and printing, but gradually these industries have declined because production and manufacturing have moved to the South and the Midwest, and even as far away as Southeast Asia. These loft buildings are now increasingly being occupied by residential tenants who enjoy the large spaces at the relatively low prices available in these buildings. In many of them, the landlords have proceeded to convert them into apartment houses and have then arranged to sell them to tenants. This of course requires the sponsor to obtain a new certificate of occupancy for residential use from the Department of

Buildings and to perform substantial renovations on the buildings. There is a strong demand for residential loft co-ops as they offer many incentives not available in standard apartments. It is not uncommon to find a loft containing upwards of 2,200 to 3,000 square feet of open space. This gives tenants freedom to create their own little worlds. Since the average suburban family house has only 1,600 square feet, many of the lofts, by comparison, offer immense amounts of space.

10

FORMS OF REAL ESTATE OWNERSHIP

Real estate ownership takes many different forms. We will now briefly review some of the more popular ones.

Individual Ownership

The simplest form of real estate ownership involves owning the property in your name, jointly with your wife, or as tenants in common with someone else. You are fully responsible for the property, and any income or loss directly affects you. If you do not want your actual name on the deed to the property, you are permitted by law to file a trade name. It should be kept in mind, however, that anyone can go down to the County Clerk's office and look up the business certificate to ascertain who is the real owner.

Partnership

You may also elect to purchase the building with a partner. You may not by yourselves have enough money to purchase a building, but together you may have enough. Also, you may need to have a partner to share in the management of the building. You and your partners may be holding down full time jobs and do not have enough time alone to run the building properly. With a partner, you have someone with whom to share the duties and responsibilities as well as someone with whom you can discuss problems as they arise. There are many different forms of partnerships and innumerable provisions can always be inserted to partnership agreements. A simple partnership agreement is inexpensive to prepare. One can purchase forms, from Blumberg/Excelsior or other legal printers that contain all the essential provisions for agreements. A certificate of Partnership must be filed with the County Clerk in the county in which you will be doing business, setting forth the names and addresses of all partners. The partnership entity pays no taxes and any income or loss produced by the property will be passed through to the individual partners. Keep in mind that partnership does not shield an investor from potential liability, and each individual partner can be held personally responsible for the entire debt obligation.

Limited Partnerships

The limited partnership is a hybrid between a corporation and a partnership. A limited partnership consists of two classes of partners, namely general partners and limited partners. The general partner in a limited partnership is the equivalent of a general partner in an ordinary partnership. He is personally responsible for all losses realized by the partnership as he has personal responsibility. The limited partner is very similar to a shareholder in a corporation. The limited partner has limited liability with respect to any losses incurred by the partnership. Should a limited partnership experience losses which are far in excess of its capital then the limited partner will only be liable to the extent of the capital in the partnership, with the general partner being liable for the remainder. One of the requirements of being a limited partner is that the limited partner may not take an active role, or have a say in the management of the partnership. The sole responsibility for the management and operation of the partnership is vested in the general partner. Should a limited partner attempt to take an active role then he will lose his limited partner status and become a general partner, with respect to third parties, and expose himself to all liabilities.

A limited partnership is like a general partnership in that all gains or losses pass through to the individual partners for tax purposes. The limited partnership itself only files an informational tax return, and is not subject to any income tax. All tax liabilities or tax deductions are passed through to the partners. Limited partnerships are very popular with tax shelters and real estate syndications as they can give the passive investors (limited partners) limited liability while being able to pass through directly to them all the allowed tax losses (which are currently subject to more stringent requirements by the Internal Revenue Service).

Corporations

A corporation is deemed to be a separate entity when it comes to taxes and liabilities. Normally, a corporation is used to shield investors from any personal liability. Also, the corporation will pay taxes on all income received and will take all tax losses for any losses sustained. Ordinary corporations cannot pass either gains or losses through to shareholders. All that such a corporation can do is to declare and pay dividends to its shareholders. These are dividends paid from the income obtained by the corporation after the payment of corporate taxes.

The corporation has a continuity of life and the shares of the corporation may be freely assigned. To obtain a partnership status, the partnership must provide that the partnership interests are not freely assignable and that the partnership has a limited life, but a corporation can continue forever. With the death or incapacity of a general partner, a partnership or limited partnership is normally dissolved. But with the death of any shareholder of the corporation, the corporation can still continue to operate. Corporations are governed by Boards of Directors which elect corporate officers. In turn, the Board of Directors is elected by the shareholders of the corporation.

There are many different kinds of corporations. You can have a corporation with just one shareholder, who will also the sole Director and officer of the corporation. Or you can have a corporation with thousands upon thousands of shareholders. A corporation will act to shield its shareholders from almost all kinds of liabilities. A shareholder cannot be liable (except under extraordinary circumstances) for the losses and liabilities incurred by a corporation. Many risky forms of property are purchased in the name of a corporation just to obtain this protection.

Corporations that elect to be taxed pursuant to Subchapter S of the Internal revenue Code are similar to partnerships in that these corporations may pass through to its shareholders all taxable gains or losses. However, a Subchapter S corporation may only have a limited number of shareholders and may not pass through losses in excess of its capital basis.

Limited Liability Companies

A new form of entity has recently been introduced in New York State, after having been established in other states. It is rapidly gaining in popularity and contains elements of a limited partnership along with those of a corporation. It is called a Limited Liability Company and has all the benefits of both a limited partnership and a corporation.

In a limited partnership, to avoid liability for the general partner, a corporation is normally used as the general partner. This enables both the limited and general partners to have limited liability. With a Limited Liability Company, there is only one class of investor and they all receive limited liability. Although this entity is quite new, it is growing rapidly in popularity and will probably replace most small limited partnerships and corporations over the next few years.

With a limited partnership you are required to publish a notice of its existence in a newspaper selected by the County Clerk, this did not have to be done with a corporation. The cost of publication alone can run between $800 to $1,600 and exceeds by far the actual cost involved in forming the limited partnership. Because you do not have to advertise when you form a corporation, the cost of setting one up is substantially less. With a Limited Liability Company you are also required to publish, and this can bring the cost of forming one to between $1,500 to $2,200, which is substantially more than the cost of forming a corporation. In the opinion of many people, a Limited Liability Company is superior to either a limited partnership or a corporation, and they are recommending that it is worth the additional cost to establish a Limited Liability Company.

Trusts

Trusts have been a common form of real estate ownership for many years. An individual may purchase an investment for his family and can own it in trust for his wife and children. As the trustee, he has full responsibility for the operation and management of the property while he can pass through all income and gains directly to the trust beneficiaries. Trusts are very flexible and there can be various allocations of income, losses and gains, with respect to the property. Trusts also offer numerous tax benefits in flexibility and planning. An individual may set up a trust where the economic benefits go to someone else but he still retains economic control over the property.

Real Estate Investment Trusts

The form of trust used within the industry is called the "Real Estate Investment Trust," and is commonly referred to as a "REIT." These trusts invest primarily in real estate and have a minimum of one hundred shareholders. Although the trust may not pass any tax losses on to the shareholders, the trust is entitled to pass through all gains to the shareholders (pursuant to Subchapter M of the Internal Revenue Code) without the trust having to pay any taxes upon the income. In other aspects, a REIT is very similar to a publicly held corporation. Almost all REITs are publicly held and enable passive investors to invest in real estate.

REITs have had a roller coaster history. When the first ones became popular about thirty years ago, they were deemed to in instant money making machines. Many of the REITs specialized in particular phases of real estate. Some REITs became strictly construction loan lenders, mortgage lenders or equity investors while others became hybrids, investing in both mortgages and real estate. The theory was that if a REIT could lend money at a greater rate of interest than that at which it borrowed, it could then proceed to earn a greater and greater income each year by borrowing more money that was then loaned out, and earn the differential. However, many of these REITs went public at about the same time, and there was a lot of money chasing a small number of projects. To invest the money, many of the REITs then made very risky loans, which resulted in tremendous losses. Many of these REITs landed up in bankruptcy, or with a market value that was but a small fraction of the price for which they had traded previously. Many large commercial banks and insurance companies sponsored REITs, making it possible for them to assume the riskier loans, which those institutions as such were not prepared to assume. Even with the sponsorship of strong financial institution many of these REITs lost substantial sums of money.

For example, Chase Manhattan Bank launched a REIT known as Chase Manhattan Mortgage and Realty Investors. The REIT went public at $20 a share and promptly went to $55 a share. After experiencing substantial losses and going through a bankruptcy reorganization, the REIT became known as the Triton Group and traded at $.75 a share. Many other REITs sponsored by large institutions suffered similar fates. It appears that the REITs relied upon financial projections rather than on actual realities. They were too concerned with calculating paper profits than with actually rolling up their sleeves and looking at the projects. Everything is cyclical and projections cannot be made on continual improvements without considering financial downturns.

In the last several years, REITs have gone through a total revitalization and many new REITs have gone public in the past few years. Many of these REITs tend to be more specialized. There are now REITs which invest just in residential housing in the Washington D.C. area. Some REITs invest only in very large regional shopping centers, and there are even those, which invest exclusively in golf courses. Many of these REITs are conservatively financed and appear to be successful.

Public Corporations

Many public corporations have been formed to hold real estate. At present this form of ownership is not particularly popular and most public entities are either master limited partnerships or REITs.

A master limited partnership is basically a very large limited partnership that trades as a public company. All income can be passed through to the partners without any taxation at the corporate level. Master limited partnerships are primarily used for natural resource investments such as oil and timber.

These public corporations are of two kinds. One has been actively involved in the construction and development of real estate, while the other was primarily concerned with passive investment. Those corporations which took an active interest in real estate tended to be more successful in their primary businesses than in real estate. The latter experienced both good and bad times depending upon economic conditions. Those corporations, which were sold to the public for the passive ownership of real estate, therefore did not do well. As the corporation's chief income was from real estate, the taxable income reported was always substantially below the actual cash flow generated by the properties. The corporation's stock, although selling at a price above its actual book value, tended to sell substantially below the actual market value of the real estate assets, which they owned. The investing public was familiar with calculating the value of a corporation on the basis of its net taxable income. Price earnings ratios (the earnings per share divided by the market price per share) was and still is a common criterion used by investors in making a quick determination whether the shares of a publicly held corporation are cheap or expensive. Cash flow and appraised book value are still not common criteria the general public can use to evaluate the purchase of common stock.

Most security analysis focuses on the quantity and quality of earnings for a public corporation and the forecasted growth of those earnings. The income statement is of primary importance with the balance sheet being used mainly to determine the quality of earnings and the ability of the corporation to sustain such earnings. Analysts focus on cash positions, accounts receivable, inventory and debts to determine whether the corporation can properly finance its sales and the inventory is turning over. The underlying assets of a public corporation are analyzed to determine how they will influence future sales. Since the overwhelming number of public corporations are involved in manufacturing and sales, these issues are relevant concerns.

Real estate entities are concerned with appreciation of assets as well as profits and cash flow. Appreciation in assets is not a primary concern for most analysts as it can be somewhat vague and does not concern most investors. Price earnings ratios are determined by estimates of future earnings growth. Investors wish to buy companies with strong earnings growth, which in turn lead to expanded price earnings ratios, which result in accelerated increases in the price of the stock.

Real estate investment entails another approach, and is not suitable for this type of analysis. It is a different breed of animal. Although there is much analysis of REITs, they primarily trade on yield.

One of the most successful publicly held real estate corporations of all time, Tishman Realty and Construction Corp., decided to liquidate rather than to continue as a publicly held corporation, traded on the New York Stock Exchange. At the time the liquidation was announced the corporation's stock was languishing at approximately $10 or $11 a share. After liquidation, the shareholders received almost $30 in cash for their stock. The principal shareholders obviously felt that there was no purpose in remaining a public entity if the public could not appreciate the value of its assets. Tishman Realty at the time of its liquidation happened to own some of the most prime office buildings available within New York City.

Even today, many publicly held real estate companies sell substantially below their actual value because they cannot demonstrate increasing earnings per share. This is particularly true of companies that own substantial amounts of undeveloped land. Two such examples are Texas Pacific Land Trust (TPL), traded on the New York Stock Exchange, and Tejon Ranch (TRC) traded on the American Stock Exchange.

TPL owns one million acres of raw land in West Texas. Each share of stock represents approximately 1/3 of an acre. There is even oil and gas on some of the land and TPL receives royalties. They also rent out their land for cattle grazing for which they receive some income. The bulk of its income though, comes from selling off the land to buyers on a gradual basis. It is commonly accepted that the stock is selling at a substantial discount to the actual value of the land and yet there has been little activity for years.

TRC owns approximately 270,000 acres of land just past commuting distance from Los Angeles. They farm the land and raise cattle. Their earnings are both small and stagnant. Plans are being made to develop the land but because of the huge size of the parcel, development is a long and slow process. Here also, most analysts believe that the shares are extremely cheap when compared with the actual value of the land. Still the stock has continued to decline with little or no interest.

11

FORMS OF FINANCING

Having considered the various forms of real estate ownership, it is important that we now discuss the various forms of financing available for the purchase of real estate.

Mortgages

The most common and prevalent way to finance real estate is to secure a loan from a lender by a mortgage or lien upon the property. In the event that the borrower defaults in making mortgage payments, then the lender or mortgagee has the security of the mortgage as collateral for the loan. The mortgagee can commence foreclosure proceedings, and eventually sell the property at public auction. In the event that no one seeks to purchase the property, then the mortgagee has the option of purchasing the property in satisfaction or partial satisfaction of its loan. There are many different kinds of mortgages.

There may be a first mortgage on property, or a second mortgage, which is subordinate to all rights and obligations of the first mortgage. It is not uncommon to find properties with three or four mortgages upon them. A mortgagee making a loan may require that the person obtaining the mortgage loan sign personally for the loan and be responsible for its repayment. The mortgagee may even insist that a third party sign the loan as well as an additional guarantee for payment. As said before, a mortgage may be self-amortizing, or have a balloon payment at the end, when it comes due. A mortgage may be for only a few months, or for many decades. The interest rate can be high or low. The mortgage may be spread over several buildings, known as a"spreader agreement" to provide additional security. The interest rate can be fixed or variable. The interest rate can be tied to the prime rate, the Federal Home Loan Board (FHLB) Index of loans, the six-month treasury bill rate, or even the London Inter Bank Rate (LIBOR). Needless to say, mortgages can vary greatly.

Leaseholds

Another form of financing is that of taking a lease on a property rather than a mortgage. For example when Wal Mart or J.C. Penny build a store, rather than obtaining mortgage financing for the store, they will sell their store to an investor and then lease the store back for a period of twenty or twenty five years with options to renew at five year intervals for an additional twenty five years. The investor becomes the landlord and the department store becomes the tenant. The department store pays rent to the landlord each month pursuant to the terms of the lease. Although this is not called a mortgage, it serves the almost identical purpose of a mortgage. Title companies, used to refer to these transactions as a deed in lieu of a mortgage. Today we call these conveyances "sale-leaseback" transactions.

Sale-leaseback transactions offer substantial benefits to both parties. The department store is able to have its store constructed and to remain in possession without having to spend any money on construction. Had it sought to obtain a conventional mortgage, it might have only obtained a mortgage for 60% or 70% of the value of the building with the rest of the cost having to be supplied by the department store. In a sale-leaseback transaction, the department stores does not spend any of its money and all the funds come from the investor. The investor acquires a mortgage secured by the lease to the department store and then supplies the additional equity capital above the financing to pay for the construction of the building. In addition, the investor is able to take depreciation on the building, which he leases to the department store. The result of this is that part of the rental income is tax-free because the depreciation expense offsets and reduces part of the investor's income. The department store then pays less in rent that it would have had to pay had it obtained its own mortgage and supplied its own equity to construct the building. At the end of twenty-five years, which is the usual life of a department store, the tenant has the option of continuing to remain in possession and to pay rent, or giving the now old building back to the investor.

Leaseholds are also extensively used by builders who are assembling sites for the construction of large office buildings. Land may not be depreciated so the builder sells the land to an investor, who receives an annual rent, and then leases back the land to construct an office building on it. (Underlying leases may or may not be subordinate to mortgages upon the actual building.) Most institutional lenders require that in making a leasehold mortgage on an office building, their mortgage have priority over the ground lease. In other words, should there be a foreclosure of the leasehold mortgage on the building, then the ownership of the fee (the land) will be subordinate to the leasehold mortgage. If the foreclosure sale does not produce enough money to pay a leasehold mortgagee, the fee interest will be wiped out. This is a risk taken by the owner of the land in leasing it back to the developer of the office building, which is subject to the financial institution's construction mortgage loan.

Equity Participation

In many instances, a developer or purchaser of real property does not have all the funds necessary to complete the transaction. The transaction may contain a great deal of risk but offer a very high reward. It may be a transaction where the mortgage financing obtainable is not sufficient and the purchaser needs additional outside funds. The purchaser may seek co-investors to invest with him in the venture. In the event that the venture fails then they will all lose their investment. In the event that the venture is a success, then all the equity participants will share in the profits.

There are many different forms of equity participation. A simple form of equity participation may simply involve calling a friend and asking him to go partners with you on the purchase of a building. You may agree that you will share the profits equally but that you will receive a management fee because of all the effort involved on your part. In many forms of equity participation, the co-investor is normally a passive investor who puts up the majority of the money. The originator of the project may only have to put up a small portion of the funds but does all the work. They would then normally agree to split the profits equally or on any other percentage basis which may be agreeable to both of them.

Many institutional investors have been seeking equity participation as a means of earning a higher return on their investments. They may consider going partners with a developer of a shopping center, office building, garden apartment complex, or health care facility. The institutional investor will put up all the money and will then agree to share the profits with the developer after the investor has first received a return on its investment equal to the return it would have received had the investment been a mortgage. For example, a developer may need one million dollars to develop a small shopping center. The institutional investor will agree to put up all the money in return for receiving 20% of the profits with a 10% return on its cash investment each year. If, after the property is developed it shows a return of $100,000.00, all the money will be allocated to the institutional investor as its 10% return. If the property shows a $200,000.00 return the year after, the institutional investor would receive $100,000.00 as its allocated interest share and an additional $20,000.00 as its share of the profits in the co-venture. The developer will receive the remaining $80,000.00 without investing any money of his own.

In many instances, a mortgagee, as a condition to giving a mortgage on property, may insist on a small equity participation in the property in addition to its mortgage payments. This is commonly called a "kicker". The lender feels that its return on its mortgage is not sufficient to fully compensate it for the risk involved and insists upon a "sweetener" for giving the mortgage loan. If the property is successful, the institutional investor will receive its mortgage payments with a percentage of the profits. The sweetener, can be in a form of a percentage of the gross rent above a certain level, a share in the actual profits above a certain level, or even an outright equity interest in the building.

Personal Financing

Many small investors find that they are unable to find institutions to lend them money after they have purchased a piece of property. Other than purchase money financing, there is no other financing available to them. To compensate for this, they may go to banks and seek to borrow money based on their own personal credit worthiness. The borrowing of the money has nothing to do with the real estate in which it is going to be invested. If the investor fails to make good on the loan he will be personally responsible.

This is a very viable approach to investors who are beginning to make their initial investments and who are purchasing properties in marginal areas where institutional mortgages cannot be obtained. They borrow money on a personal basis and use the money either for the acquisition of property or for its improvement. As they pay back the personal loan they continue to gain credit worthiness at the bank and are able to borrow more and more money each time. As time progresses they may be able to move up and purchase better properties for which they will be able to obtain institutional financing.

Government Assisted Financing

The United States Government and local municipalities are another source of funds for property in marginal and distressed areas. Through various programs, the government is prepared to lend money to investors seeking to renovate low-income housing. Many of these loans are at extremely low interest rates and for long periods of time. The terms of these loans are always favorable as they are an inducement to investors to renovate this kind of distressed property.

One problem with this area is that a substantial amount of red tape is often involved in obtaining government assisted financing. Normally, numerous forms must be dealt with and filled out and substantial numbers of interviews and conferences are required. Obtaining government assisted financing can be very complex and require the assistance of specialists in this area, which can also be costly. Even after the loan is approved, the municipality or governmental agency giving the loan may not have required funding to make good on the loan commitment.

12

STRATEGIES FOR REAL ESTATE INVESTING

There are various strategies available for the real estate investor in achieving his goal and accumulating assets. Outlined below are several strategies available to the ordinary investor. None of these strategies is very complex and most of them involve plain common sense. I have tried to present diametrically opposed strategies so that each individual can understand the basis of each strategy. These strategies are not intended to make the individual wealthy, but are intended to highlight various approaches and concepts, which are necessary for developing a successful strategy.

Purchasing land or vacant buildings in distressed areas

One approach would be to purchase vacant land in the South or East areas of the Bronx, in the Northern part of Manhattan or in the Northeastern portion of Brooklyn. This land is available for very reasonable prices. The cost of purchasing these vacant lots are little more than what it would cost to purchase something similar in many parts of Upstate New York which are very rural. These vacant lots in New York City are near living thriving areas, namely, the central business districts of the boroughs and of Manhattan. These depressed areas are readily accessible by rapid transit, subways, buses and highways to all the essential areas of operation within the City of New York. At one time these neighborhoods were thriving communities containing both successful residential and commercial structures.

Needless to say these areas are now disasters. Although it appears unlikely they will develop in the near future, it does appear plausible that these areas will again be redeveloped. If investors can purchase raw land in obscure rural areas or even forests, there is no reason why this urban land should not be appealing for the same reasons.

I am recommending the purchase of land or vacant buildings, as the average real estate investor is not prepared or equipped to cope with the problems of providing essential services to tenants in these areas. Once the land or vacant building is acquired, the investor's sole concern will be with placing adequate insurance upon the property and arranging for the property to be kept clean and for any and all vagrants and squatters to be removed from the property.

Purchasing a Home just Outside the Commuting Range

Another approach is to purchase a home, which is presently not appealing to commuters. In purchasing these homes, the buyer is able to obtain extreme value for his money. He will be able to buy a much larger and well built home that he would normally be able to afford. The home will also come with substantially more land than would be available in an area close to the City.

Many purchasers of homes such as these, regard the additional traveling time to and from work in the City, as their second job. It is because of this additional traveling time that they are able to purchase such magnificent homes. Additionally, many purchasers of homes in outlying areas believe that these outlying areas will develop into communities and that other business and commercial centers will develop closer to these communities than to the City.

With the acceleration of technology, more and more people are working out of their homes either operating their own businesses or being affiliated with a large corporations which does not require them to report daily to the office. With computers, modems and faxes, it has become easier for many individuals to work out of their homes.

Areas such as these lie in Upstate New York, Eastern Suffolk County and Southern New Jersey. Homes in these areas can be purchased for very reasonable prices and offer a substantial chance for appreciation. Numerous small commercial centers are developing outside of New York City and these commercial centers are attracting employees to these outlying areas. The growth and development of the Northern parts of Westchester County and the Southern portions of Putnam and Dutchess Counties. The development of Route 110 in Melville, Long Island as aided the development of such residential areas as St. James and Stony Brook in Suffolk County.

Buying a Building with High Financial Leverage

The classic approach to real estate investment with little money is that of purchasing a building with a high mortgage and low cash, borrowing from all your friends and relatives and then trying to work down the loan. If the purchaser makes the right buy then the property's income will increase and he will have money available to pay back all the loans and mortgages. However, should there be a slight fluctuation or downturn, he will be very disappointed and be wiped out.

This has always been the classic approach to investment. The purchaser borrows at fixed rates of interest and purchases a property showing an increasing variable return. Once the purchase is made, the investor knows that the cost of loan payments cannot increase. Yet he is hopeful that income will continue to go up. Although the property initially may just produce enough income to satisfy the interest payments on the loans, it is anticipated that the income will increase to the point that it will be sufficient for the investor to commence paying back the principal on these loans and even to provide some money for the investor.

Trading up houses, co-ops and condos

A very common and historically successful approach is the purchase of a small house, co-op or condo, selling it and using the cash received to purchase a more expensive one. Initially, the purchaser may but a small studio apartment for $150,000.00 with $30,000.00 cash down and the balance by obtaining a loan from a bank in the sum of $120,000.00. After a few years, the apartment may be worth $200,000.00 and the loan reduced to $100,000.00, leaving the purchaser with $100,000.00 in equity. The purchaser will then take the $100,000.00 and purchase an apartment for $500,000.00 by obtaining a new $400,000 purchase money mortgage from the bank. This procedure will be repeated by the purchaser every few years with each time the purchaser buying a larger or better located piece of property.

Buying a run down Brownstone

Another very commonly used approach is that of buying a run down brownstone in an upwardly changing neighborhood and fixing it up yourself. You do not have to do the work yourself but can act as a general contractor in hiring workers.

The advantage of doing this are two fold. As the neighborhood continues to improve, the value of the property will continue to increase. Furthermore, the improvements you make in the property will only add to the increase in value. With the passing of time, because of the shortages of workers and materials, the costs of replicating these improvements will increase substantially. As time passes and as you continue to do the work, you will learn all about the repairs and improvements, which have to be made, and how to deal with hired help.

This work can be very troublesome as no work is ever done on time or for the cost originally anticipated. There are normal foul-ups with any construction work and the cost normally exceeds the amount, which you budgeted. If you are living in a brownstone at the time you are making the improvements, your life can become very hectic and it can become the equivalent of a full time job. Nothing ever goes right with construction and problems always develop. You may find yourself without water and heat for days at a time. Doing a job such as this requires a substantial commitment of time and energy on your part. You will be continually bothered by various municipal agencies and you will have to keep on top of your sub-contractors and workers. Another danger in this approach is that you may find yourself spending more money than you would be able to recover upon the immediate sale of this property.

By living in the house during construction you will be saving having to pay rent or maintain another and separate residence. Also, most workers show up very early in the morning for the job and if you live there it is easier to greet them when they arrive at 7:00 a.m.

In general though, this has been a successful approach for most purchasers of real estate. When they are finished renovating the brownstone, they have normally done it for a cheaper price that would have been obtainable from a general building contractor. Furthermore, constant supervision of the work, results in a superior job.

Investing with an Active Participant

It might pay for you, if you do not have the time, to find someone actively involved in real estate and invest with him. Your plumber may want to but a building but may not have the necessary money. The superintendent of your building may want to buy a building in another area but needs someone to finance him. By acting as the non-active partner in supplying the necessary funds, you may find yourself obtaining a worthwhile investment. Of course, it is very important to know the person with whom you are investing. Not only are you investing in a building but you are actually investing in the individual whom you are trusting with your money. It is an important to know the person as it is to know the property.

By investing with someone who can actively run the property, you may be able to relieve a big burden from your shoulders in not having to be concerned with the day-to-day operation of the property. The person with whom you are investing may be able to make the necessary repairs for which you would have had to hire another person to do. Better do deal with someone who is too honest than someone who is too smart. There are a lot of fast talkers out there and you must be very careful if you wish to reserve your money.

Finding Someone to Finance You

The alternate approach to the above, is to find someone to finance your purchase of real estate, with you doing all the work. You may find an excellent investment but not have the money with which to purchase it. You should consider approaching your family, friends and co-workers. If they know you and trust you, they may be willing to invest money with you.

An additional benefit of this approach, is that you have access to other minds in making determinations. One of your investors may be an accountant or a lawyer whom you can approach for accounting and legal advice. Normally, you will be able to obtain this advice free of charge, and you can be certain of the accuracy of this advise as the persons giving it has a financial stake in the outcome. If you are successful with your initial investment, you will find it easier to attract outside investors the next time. Of course, if your investment fails, you will have to continue seeing these people afterwards and may be embarrassed by what has occurred.

Working as a Real Estate Sales Person

A very good approach for getting started in real estate is getting a part-time or full-time job as a real estate sales person with a licensed real estate broker. This approach gives you the dual opportunity of meeting people and learning the business. By showing various properties to individuals you are able to gain some insight into their thinking. Their criticism of a property to you may accurately reflect the reality of the situation or may just be an attempt to bargain down the price. After showing various buildings within the same neighborhood to potential purchasers, you will gradually learn what the acceptable and going price ranges are and which properties are considered more attractive that other.

Be aware, however, that working as a real estate salesperson can be very frustrating as well. You may have to show a potential property to many purchasers before you can generate any offers. You may then obtain an offer for a certain property and communicate this offer to the seller only to learn that another salesman has brought a competing offer at a slightly higher price. You can come close to making a sale many times only to lose out at the very last moment.

Speculating on Mortgages

Another approach, which can be more passive than the other involves the purchasing of mortgages on real property as an investment. Many individuals take back purchase money mortgage loans when they sell their property. The individuals may then need the money and wish to sell the mortgage loan. As this is not a fluid market, these mortgages are normally sold at substantially discounted prices and offer high rates in interest.

As each mortgage loan is in a different amount and on a different property, there is no marketplace for the loan. Each purchase is negotiable between buyer and seller. There is very fluid and market place for securitized mortgage loans but this is not relevant to our situation. Of course, the rate of interest on the mortgage purchased, depends upon the security and safety of the mortgage. A first mortgage will normally bear a lower rate of interest than a second mortgage. If the investor ascertains that the building is a good building and will produce substantial income to support the mortgage payments, he may consider purchasing the existing mortgage on the property from the individual offering it for sale. Once the mortgage is purchased, the investor need only sit back and wait for his payments to be received. You need not be a bank to service and receive income on a mortgage loan.

Problems can develop, if the mortgagor or borrower, is late in his payments or falls behind in making them. The owner of the property may be mismanaging the building and therefore not generating the income necessary for servicing and paying the mortgages upon the property. When this happens, the investor will have to assume an active role and proceed to enforce his rights as mortgagee. He may go down and speak to the owner and try to work it out with him, or he may retain an attorney and commence foreclosure proceedings to obtain title to the property and to enforce the default, which has occurred under the terms of the mortgage loan. This can be a very messy situation and require a substantial amount of time and effort. It can also be very aggravating as the owner of the property will fight tooth and nail to keep his building.

The more speculative the mortgage, the greater the chance of a default occurring. If the mortgage is extremely safe and secure, then there is little chance of foreclosure. A "seasoned mortgage" is a mortgage, which has been in existence for some time and upon which payments of interest and principal have been regularly received. These mortgages are considered relatively safe as there is already a history of the mortgagor or owner of the property making payments in reduction of the original amount of the mortgage. In addition the value of the property my have increased since the mortgage was placed on it. Normally a seasoned mortgage is considered more secure than a new mortgage.

Buying with Friends

Many investors in publicly held securities have joined investment clubs so that they might make investments with friends. Likewise, many initial investors in real estate have gotten together with friends and pooled their money in making their first investment. This is a good approach as you and your friends have the opportunity of learning together. It also gives you the comfort of not being alone in making the investment and having other people to speak with. By working together, you and your friends can talk over all decisions that are made and share the responsibility. It is important that the friends you invest with are reliable and trustworthy.

It is very common that in many such ventures all the work falls on one of the parties who often does all the work without adequate remuneration. If you are going to do the work, make sure that you receive proper financial remuneration for doing so. It can be in the form of a management fee, payments based on the time involved, or by receiving a larger share of the pot. If you do not receive any additional financial incentive then you may become lax and the work will not get done. Buying a building is not like buying shares of stock in a corporation. The property must be maintained and managed. It's a job and someone has to do it.

Buying Ancillary to your Business

A very common approach is for the storekeeper to purchase the building in which his store is located. The primary concern is the protection of the business from not being forced to relocate at the time of the lease expiration. Many small owners of businesses find themselves in serious trouble, when their landlord either elects not to renew their lease, seeks a high increase in rent, or sells the building to another user who needs the space for his own purposes.

The storekeeper also feels that he has expended many thousands of dollars in renovating his store and making it attractive. The money lavished on the store has also improved the quality of the building. Furthermore, the storekeeper wants the building to look nice and add to the appeal of the storefront. To accomplish these goals many storekeepers have purchased the buildings in which these stores are located.

This approach not only applies to the storekeepers. A factory owner may decide to purchase the small factory building so that he will have additional space for expansion should that become necessary. Also, by owing the building, the factory owner need not worry about his lease expiring and being forced to move. Because the storekeeper and factory owner are at their place of business every day, they can carefully watch and maintain their buildings. A disadvantage to this, however is that they will always be available to tenants who may want to complain.

Buying with Someone Knowledgeable

Lastly, you may consider investing your money with someone you consider knowledgeable. This is a very broad area and encompasses many situations. You may consider approaching someone who has a reputation for being successful in real estate and offer him money to invest on your behalf. You may consider purchasing a participation in a limited partnership being offered by an investment group. You may even consider purchasing shares of stock in a Real Estate Investment Trust or in a publicly held real estate development company.

Needless to say, one pays a price to invest with someone knowledgeable. If you invest is a limited partnership, you will find that the general partner and the salesman (who may be affiliated with a large brokerage concern) will take multiple fees and charges. In publicly offered limited partnerships various fees are received by the general partner, the organizer, the accounting and law firms, the managing agent, and the sales organization responsible for putting the project together. It is very important to inquire as to what the profit-sharing arrangement is with the general partner and as to what the fees and disbursements are being paid from your investment funds.

In making this kind of investment, you must know something about the organization that you are investing with. It is more important to know with whom you are investing, than what you are investing in. As you are seeking someone with knowledge, it is not for you to question the nature of the investment. Your questioning should be limited to inquiring about the competence of the person with whom you are entrusting your funds. You must look into the history of the individual's organization. It is very easy for someone to produce paper projections of a successful project. It is actually more difficult to deliver a successful investment.

13

LABELS, ERRORS AND DEFINITIONS

It is the nature of our reality that we assign labels to various roles and then assume the role will correspond with the label. When we refer to an entity as a tenant we assume that the entity will then assume and perform the role of a tenant. Real estate today has gone through massive changes and many of the labels and definitions, which we use to describe the various relationships, are inaccurate or completely erroneous.

In a sale-leaseback transaction where a department store will sell the land and building to the investor and then lease it back for a lengthy period of time, we still refer to the department store as the tenant and the investor as the landlord. The department store is responsible for the maintenance and operation of its store and of the property. The department store has a lease to occupy the property for a length of time, which corresponds to the basic economic life of the building. The discounted time value of the residual asset (the building after the expiration of the lease and all renewals) after fifty years is almost negligible. If the property will be worth $1,500,000.00 after fifty years, its present value at current interest rates is approximately $40,000.00. In reality, the department store is not the tenant but the actual owner of the property. The department store does not really have a lease with the owner, it has a mortgage. This is in reality of one of a lender and a borrower. Although we use the terms landlord and tenant in describing this relationship, these terms are erroneous and will lead to erroneous thinking on the part of the investor contemplating the transaction.

Many apartment buildings in distressed areas are purchased for small amounts of cash but with large mortgages. The purchaser, with a small amount of money, becomes the owner of the building while the mortgagee becomes the holder of a substantial money mortgage loan on the premises. The purchaser of the building will have to pay more in mortgage payments to the seller than what he actually receives for himself after the payment of all expenses. The overwhelming bulk of the equity in the building is still owned by the seller by reason of his mortgage, than by the purchaser.

It is wrong, in a situation such as this, to refer to the purchaser of the property as the owner and to the seller as the mortgagee. In reality, the new owner of the property is acting as the managing agent for the seller who has the highest equity investment in the building. The new owner of the building is paying more money to the old owner (in the form of mortgage payments) than he is receiving for himself. All the work is being done by the purchaser while the bulk of the income is being received by the seller. The purchaser is acting as the managing agent for the seller and receiving a small management fee based upon the economic performance of the building. This same situation may also be looked at as a long-term lease, with the cash payment towards the purchase price being regarded as the tenant's security lease deposit. These examples show how unstable or insecure the relationship is in reality.

The concept of return also has various definitions. Do you consider the return on a real estate investment to be cash received after the payment of all expenses. Does the appreciation of the property calculate into the actual cash return? Should the amortization of the unpaid mortgage principal also be included? Should tax benefits be included? This sort of evaluation is full of vague areas.

Obviously, the concept of return has a different definition to each investor. Many investors regard the actual cash on cash return as the only true criteria for calculating return. Others will look to include amortization of debt, tax benefits and even appreciation (which is very hard to judge on an annual basis).

The determination of a definition of return is necessary before a decision is made whether or not a building is suitable for investment. To different investors, the same building showing the same identical cash flow statement, may or may not be suitable for investment. Would purchase a building showing negative cash flow but rapid amortization or mortgage principal? Would you but a building showing substantial cash flow but with little chance for appreciation and a strong possibility for depreciation? Would you purchase a building that just breaks even with a substantial cash requirement but which has excellent potential for appreciation while offering some tax benefits?

Many experts will tell you that you have to factor in all the numbers and go by the net result. Obviously, you should purchase a building based on the figures. If the cash flow far exceeds the possible decline in value, it's a good investment. And yet many investors will not operate on figures alone but insist on other criteria. They will not buy a building, which can decline in value because they feel strongly that the key to success is in buildings that appreciate. Even with the temptation of substantial cash flow, they will not make such an investment. Likewise, many investors insist that each building should carry itself and will never purchase a building that does not show positive cash flow.

The above examples are given to highlight the fact that in making any real estate investment, the investor must look beyond the labels and definitions and decide for himself whether or not the building is suitable for his investment. This is a personal decision and should be given much thought before buying. As has been said, buying is fast, selling is slow. Go slow before buying. You may own your purchase for a long time, whether you like it or not.

14

REAL ESTATE FORMS

Real property cannot be moved as it is attached to the ground. Because of this real property is brought and sold through documents.

I would like to mention and review several of the more common documents used in connection with real estate transactions.

Legal documents may be obtained from various sources. Most common documents are obtained from title companies, real estate boards, municipalities and printers of legal forms. These are not "do it yourself" forms and they should be prepared by an attorney, who is more familiar with these matters. Many attorneys have their own typed "riders" which they use to further modify these printed forms.

CONTRACTS FOR SALE OF REAL PROPERTY

The first step in purchasing real property is entering into a Contract of Sale. Once the contract is signed, you have a binding agreement.

Only when a contract is signed can you proceed to seek a mortgage loan to help finance you purchase the property. A title report is usually ordered after the contract is signed in preparation for the closing.

There are standardized contract forms available from legal printers and title companies. The contract form for a one or two family home generally contains a mortgage contingency on the purchaser being able to obtain a mortgage loan from a bank or mortgage broker. If a loan commitment is not obtained, usually within 30 to 45 days, then the purchaser can cancel the contract and obtain a refund of his deposit on contract, which is usually 10% of the purchase price. This deposit is usually held by the attorney for the seller in an interest bearing account, for the benefit of the seller.

Contracts for the purchase of commercial property and apartment houses are usually more detailed. They deal with municipal violations and the status of the tenancies in the building. Attorneys generally have their own forms, called "riders" which they attach to these contracts.

A different form of contract is used when purchasing a co-operative apartment which consists of shares of stock in the co-op and a proprietary lease to your apartment. The contract is not only contingent upon obtaining a bank loan but also on obtaining the approval of the Board of Directors of the Co-op. Each purchaser must submit an application to the Co-op and then is interviewed by the Board.

The Board of Directors of a co-operative corporation may accept or reject any prospective purchaser without reason provided there is no discrimination. A purchase of an apartment from a sponsor, one who first converted the building to co-operative ownership, need not obtain Board approval.

Each condominium unit is considered a separate piece of real estate and has its own legal description. There are special real estate forms relating to their sale as they are not co-ops but they are also not like a single family home. You receive a deed when you purchase a condominium.

CLOSING DOCUMENTS

The closing represents the actual transfer of ownership. There are various documents involved in a closing. I am including several of the more important documents.

The most commonly used Deed is a Bargain and Sale Deed with a Covenant Against Grantor's Acts. Transfer taxes are imposed on the seller by both New York City and New York State. A mansion tax is imposed on the purchaser of a private residence in excess of $1,000,000.00 by the State of New York.

Other forms of Deeds, which are used in certain circumstances, are:

Full Warranty Deeds
Quit Claim Deeds
Foreclosure Deeds
Executors Deeds

In New York City the following documents will also be required at closing:

NYC real property transfer tax return
NYS real property transfer tax return
Smoke detector affidavit
Non-foreign resident certification (for seller)

Affidavit of Non-multiple Dwelling or filing of a Multiple Dwelling Registration.

If a party to the transaction is not going to be present, then there must be a Power of Attorney given to someone who is present, so that the documents may be executed.

MORTGAGE DOCUMENTS

As said before in this book, a mortgage loan consists of a note, which is the promise to pay and the mortgage, which places a lien on the property as security for the loan.

When you borrow money from a lender or a bank, you will sign numerous other documents and papers.

The most important documents are the Note and Mortgage. The lender may also take a security interest in the personal property on the premises and require that you sign a security agreement and UCC-1 financing statement. Federal law requires all parties to sign a Real Estate Settlement Procedure Act (RESPA) statement, which sets down all costs and expenses incurred by both parties in a consumer transaction.

An Extension Agreement is used when both parties wish to extend the life of the mortgage. A Satisfaction is recorded when the mortgage loan is paid off and satisfied. A Lienor's Estoppel Certificate is needed when you need to establish either to a purchaser or secondary lender, the actual unpaid balance on the existing mortgage loan.

LEASES

There are many different forms of lease agreements in New York. I highly recommend that you use the Real Estate Board forms, as they are the most inclusive. Most of the language contained in these forms have been litigated and there is judicial precedent as to their meaning. They are also the most common variation in use today.

The Real Estate Board forms are relatively expensive and it does not pay to skimp. They are the best. They can be purchased by mail or telephone from the Real Estate Board of New York, which is situated in Manhattan.

Among the more commonly used lease forms in New York, are the following leases:

Apartments, which are subject to rent stabilization—you, must attach extensive riders, which comply with the Rent Stabilization Guidelines.

Apartments which are not subject to any rent regulations-these are simpler forms and you have more flexibility. Most common in two family homes.

Stores—including riders stating that the tenant is responsible for keeping his sidewalk clean.

Lofts and industrials spaces—landlord provides few if any services.

Offices—landlord is usually responsible for cleaning and maintenance.

The following forms also relate to lease and are readily available: Assignment of lease, Sublease agreement, Extension of lease and Surrender agreement

LANDLORD AND TENANT PROCEEDINGS

If you are operating real estate, there may be times when you will have issues with your tenants. The Landlord & Tenant Part of the Civil Court is a specialized judicial unit which handles dispute, with both residential and commercial tenants.

There are two basic kinds of proceedings. Non-payment proceedings relate to the non-payment of rent. Holdover proceedings relate to other breaches of the lease agreement such as subletting or assigning the lease without the landlord's consent.

The primary documents, which commence these proceedings, are known as the Notice of Petition and Petition. Different forms are used for non-payment and holdover proceedings. Different forms are used for commercial and residential. Almost all holdover proceedings require a Notice to Cure and a Notice of termination be served prior to the Petition and for these Notices to be annexed to the Petition.

The following forms are the most common and readily available from a commercial stationery store: 30 day Demand for Rent, 30 Notice of Termination, Notice of Petition and Petition for residential non-payment, Notice of Petition and Petition for commercial non-payment and Notice of Petition and Petition for Holdover proceeding

15

PRESENT TIMES

New York City is presently experiencing "boom" times. All segments of the real estate market are experiencing a price explosion. In Manhattan the prices of apartments and offices are at record levels. Rents have become prohibitive for both working or living. There has been a slowing, which started prior to September 11th, and appears to be continuing. We really do not know what the full impact will be of the incident, although I must believe that it will not enhance the present situation. New York City has weathered many prior catastrophes and will continue to survive.

From 1987-1992, the real estate industry in New York was in a state of decline. Some of this decline was caused by general factors, such as the changes in the tax law, which were negative to real estate investors, the massive over-building of office buildings throughout the United States, and the decline of manufacturing nationwide. Some of these factors were local, such as the shifting of white collar clerical jobs to other localities such as the South and Northwest due to lower salary scales, the demise of the printing and garment industries due to off-shore manufacturing, larger printing facilities outside of New York and the expanded technology of desk top publishing.

The decline stopped in 1992-1993 and prices stabilized and began to rise. A tremendous shortage of apartments for both ownership and rental began to develop. This was because there has been little residential construction over the part several years and more and more people are seeking to live in the urban center.

After World War II, the suburbs began to boom. The infrastructure had expanded with the construction of the Long Island Expressway, New York State Thruway and the general highway system that developed during the depression and expanded with the construction of bridges and tunnels. New technology and the long-term growth of intermodal transportation helped develop a modern subway system and commuter railroad system. Housing conditions in the City for the already long established immigrant groups were horrendous and the suburbs offered light, air and space with a place to raise happy and healthy families. New suburban communities developed and flourished while the older urban neighborhoods suffered the pangs of death. This trend continued from the mid 1940s to the mid 1970s.

By that time the generation raised in the suburbs began to experience a sense of disillusionment. The suburbs began to have problems. Commuting was taking up a greater part of the workday. The wonderful infrastructure constructed during the depression and post war years was beginning to age and was experiencing problems. There was nothing to do in the suburbs and, although isolated from the worst aspects of City life, suburbanites were also isolated from the good the City had to offer. Boredom began to become a serious problem leading to increased use of drugs and crime in the suburbs.

A slow but barely noticed migration began from the suburbs to the City in the early 1970s. Areas of the City that had been in a total state of decline began to be reborn with the movement back. The first areas to realize this gentrification were the previously established areas, which had existing structures and institutions such as Brooklyn Heights and the Upper West Side, as we had indicated previously. As the movement has gained stream, other areas have also experienced growth and development as middle-class environments. Among these communities that have already matured are Park Slope, the West Village, Hoboken, Carnegie Hill and Riverdale.

The trend towards residential living in the City has been for almost thirty years now, and appears certain to continue. Urban life now offers advantage over living in the suburbs. Commuting is easier and with both husband and wife working leaving more time to be home with the family. A woman can have both a career and a family without having to expend three hours a day commuting, which is not so inexpensive. Whether you drive or take public transportation, it has become a major expense. The real estate tax base is lower in New York City and there are numerous school available that offer a superior educational environment. There are good things in the City for children too, which cannot readily be experienced in the suburbs. They range from museums, places of higher learning, concert halls, galleries and bookstores.

Prior to 1980, the City appeared to be shrinking commercially. At one time there were numerous thriving commercial districts throughout the City, such as Court Street in Brooklyn, East 149th Street in the Bronx and Queens Plaza in Queens. These areas have shrunk noticeably. Even in Manhattan, it appears that Downtown with its older office buildings is giving way to midtown. Those who used to be referred to as "Wall Street" lawyers are now primarily located in Mid-Town. Substantial ancillary business districts existed between Downtown and Midtown but these areas have not prospered for many years. Many of the small commercial and quasi-industrial loft buildings have become primarily residential. New residential areas such as Tribeca (triangle below Canal Street) and Soho (South of Houston Street) have been created from ruined commercial districts.

New York has now become the undisputed financial center of the world and is likely to continue so in spite of September 11th. The financial sector has grown and prospered and more than compensated for the declining garment and printing industries. The money generated from the financial institutions have made a generation of young men and women rich, which in turn has produced a plethora of high end retail stores. Madison Avenue and East 57th Street are the two main Streets for luxury retail shopping.

With its growth as a financial center, numerous ancillary industries have also flourished. This includes law firms, accountants, advertising agencies, public relations, marketing, media buying and executive recruitment firms. This in turn, has lead to further high paying jobs and an enormous demand for good housing.

At present there is a great shortage of office and residential space in the City. The growing financial sector and its ancillary industries have an insatiable demand and the high price talented being hired by these firms all need places to live. This has caused a general explosion in real estate prices.

Lastly, there has been a sudden growth in technological startups in the City centered or related to the internet. We now have "Silicon Alley" and many small (and not so small) high tech firms. This rose quickly and declined even quicker with the collapse of the dot.com frenzy. Technology and the internet are here to stay and we are seeing the birthing pains of a new industry.

At this very moment a softening of the real estate market has started. The weakness began prior to September 11th and is presently continuing. It may be a temporary setback or a cyclical change. Only time can tell.

Change will continue and it must be accepted. In purchasing real estate, it is important to prepare for the bad times as it is to benefit from the good times. Money has been made and money has been lost in real estate. Although timing is extremely important, staying power is even more essential. Change does not happen quickly and trends can be seen. Once a trend starts it tend to continue. Fear can be an enemy and lead to procrastination and inertia. You must step forward and start. Thinking and planning is not enough. You must go out and do it. Do not be a hero—be careful and you will succeed.

0-595-27742-X

Made in the USA
Lexington, KY
16 November 2014